Texas Trails & Glass Pyramids

Texas Trails & Glass Pyramids

CREATING THE SAN ANTONIO BOTANICAL GARDEN

Lewis F. Fisher

FOREWORD BY Barney L. Lipscomb

MAVERICK BOOKS | TRINITY UNIVERSITY PRESS

COPUBLISHED WITH THE SAN ANTONIO BOTANICAL GARDEN

Published by
Maverick Books, an imprint of Trinity University Press
San Antonio, Texas 78212
and the San Antonio Botanical Garden

Book design by Anne Richmond Boston
Cover photo by JoMando Cruz
Author photo by Mary M. Fisher

ISBN 978-1-59534-340-6 hardcover
ISBN 978-1-59534-341-3 ebook

Trinity University Press strives to produce its books using methods and materials in an environmentally sensitive manner. We favor working with manufacturers that practice sustainable management of all natural resources, produce paper using recycled stock, and manage forests with the best possible practices for people, biodiversity, and sustainability. The press is a member of the Green Press Initiative, a nonprofit program dedicated to supporting publishers in their efforts to reduce their impacts on endangered forests, climate change, and forest-dependent communities.

The paper used in this publication meets the minimum requirements of the American National Standard for Information Sciences—Permanence of Paper for Printed Library Materials, ansi 39.48–1992.

Printed in Canada

CIP data on file at the Library of Congress
30 29 28 27 26 | 5 4 3 2 1

FRONTISPIECE: A tempietto tops the overlook near the Lucile Halsell Conservatory.

Contents

Foreword, by Barney L. Lipscomb vii
Preface viii
Introduction: A Conservatory Unlike Any Other xi

The Quest for a Botanical Garden 1
A Dozen Tries since 1884 3
A Reservoir in Washington Heights 11
The Curious Case of Mahncke Park 19

Shaping the Botanical Garden 27
Preparing the Site 29
Launching the San Antonio Botanical Garden 41
Kumamoto En and a Carriage House 51

Making a Mark on the Botanical World 61
The Moy Grande Leads the Way 63
Complications and Renewal 73
A Lively Place 83
Independent at Last 91

Map 101
Notes 102
Selected Bibliography 111
Credits 112
Index 113

The San Antonio Botanical Garden celebrates plants with panache.

Foreword

BARNEY L. LIPSCOMB

The world's botanical gardens are living collections of plants. As places of beauty and inspiration alone they contribute to human well-being. But often, like the San Antonio Botanical Garden, they are also important educational and teaching centers, performing research in botany and horticulture and promoting plant diversity and the importance of plant conservation.

Botanical gardens are also testaments to their founders' passion. Lewis F. Fisher tells the story of the struggles, successes, and disappointments of the San Antonio Botanical Garden and its heroes—gardeners, botanists, directors, educators, benefactors, volunteers—who have explored, discovered, collected, interpreted, grown, nourished, and conserved plant life. Their dreams, hopes, and hard work have made the garden a significant institution for San Antonians and for those far beyond.

As a practicing botanist, I found it gratifying to read about many of my personal research botanist friends who have played or are playing a role in the garden's plant development and conservation and the related scientific, educational, and aesthetic aspects. They include Delbert Weniger, Patty Leslie Pasztor, Toney Keeney, Paul Cox, and Michael Eason.

Conservation is a shared responsibility of governments, organizations, and individuals. Thus I read with special interest about the garden's collaboration with the Native Plant Rescue Project that saved plants from more than eighty sites doomed for development, and the garden's new and innovative Texas Recovery for Ecological and Environmental Stability initiative to rehabilitate damaged areas of native plants and trees.

I look forward to seeing the garden's planned Southwest botanical research facility come to fruition. The facility will feature classrooms, research space, and a regional seed bank, herbarium, and botanical library.

As this book suggests, the momentum of the San Antonio Botanical Garden's past achievements is moving it forward into an even more notable future.

Preface

The story of the San Antonio Botanical Garden is one of an institution whose time had come. For nearly a century calls for a botanical garden kept arising in San Antonio, but it was not until the 1960s that a group of garden clubs got the formula and politics right.

What made this garden excel was the early involvement of a well-connected San Antonian, Gilbert Denman Jr., who stepped in when initial efforts stalled in 1974. He not only came up with private funds to get things moving but worked through a botanical society he organized to be sure garden development stayed on a high plane. He kept at it behind the scenes for more than twenty-five years, as national accolades for the garden came in.

When the San Antonio Botanical Garden opened at the eastern end of Mahncke Park in 1980 it was designated the San Antonio Botanical Center. The name changed to San Antonio Botanical Gardens in 1992 and, six years later, to San Antonio Botanical Garden, singular. For clarity and consistency, I refer to the garden throughout as the San Antonio Botanical Garden. Its supporting group incorporated as the San Antonio Botanical Center Society, changed names in the same sequence, and is referred to here simply as the San Antonio Botanical Society.

It was over coffee in November 2023 that Katherine Trumble, president and CEO of the San Antonio Botanical Garden, suggested that I write this book. I was an early board member, my wife followed me, and our older son was a board member at the time. I had just completed a book on Brackenridge Park down the

hill. As with the history of that park, the origins and evolution of the garden and its Mahncke Park home turned out to differ from what was commonly believed.

For help on this project I am particularly grateful to Gregg Eckhardt at the San Antonio Water System and local historian Maria Watson Pfeiffer for their input on the early history of the garden's site. Andrew Labay, the garden's chief mission officer; Michael Eason, vice president of conservation; and longtime garden staff member Scott Litchke all provided valuable insights. Photo curator Tom Shelton at the University of Texas at San Antonio Special Collections yet again showed his unmatched ability to turn up seldom-seen images. Peggy Jones, recent president of the San Antonio Garden Center, and Rhonda Banuelos, the office manager, dug through the scrapbooks of that group, which sponsored the botanical garden.

My son Bill provided perceptive fixes, and his younger brother, Maverick (both alumni of the garden's first children's gardening sessions), and my wife, Mary, who shared splendid photographs she has taken over the years, offered additional edits. Also quite helpful were two-time botanical society board president Claire Alexander and former botanical society general manager Candace Andrews, who reviewed the manuscript; Tom Payton, former director of Trinity University Press, who encouraged this book's publication; and Trinity University Press's managing editor Sarah Nawrocki and acquisitions editor Steffanie Stevens, who helped shepherd the work through the publication process. Emily Jerman Schuster provided her expertise in editorial fine tuning, and Anne Richmond Boston her flair for distinctive book design.

One leading critic wrote that the Lucile Halsell Conservancy was "unlike any conservatory ever built."

Introduction

A CONSERVATORY UNLIKE ANY OTHER

In 1988 a resplendence of towering glass cones and pyramids emerged in an expanse of manicured gardens on a once barren bluff overlooking San Antonio. The stunning project brought international acclaim to the city and its new botanical garden.

In the last quarter of the nineteenth century a stone reservoir key to transforming San Antonio into a modern city first occupied a plot on that high ground. Later the area became part of a municipal park, but the city ignored the scraggly section and twice tried to give it away. In the 1960s a federation of garden clubs picked it as the improbable location for the botanical garden San Antonians had been trying to establish somewhere since the 1880s.

That plan became reality in 1980, when the city opened the San Antonio Botanical Garden on the bluff. Given the meager resources of the Parks and Recreation Department, which first operated the garden, the thirty-two acres seemed destined to become little more than another city park. But Gilbert Denman Jr., chair of the local nonprofit Ewing Halsell Foundation, had a grander vision.

Denman's efforts over more than a quarter century profoundly impacted the botanical garden, accomplishing far beyond what city budgets alone would allow. In 1974 he got the stalled project moving. As the garden opened in 1980, he was already searching the country for an architect who could design a major conservatory, rather than settling for the parks department's modest plan for four rooms under a metal roof. Seven months after the garden opened, the nonprofit San Antonio Botanical Society Denman had organized was chartered, and he became the official head of the architect search.[1]

The arc of the conservatory's evolution from unlikely concept to architectural triumph parallels that of the San Antonio Botanical Garden itself, as it rejected mediocrity in the pursuit of excellence and has become one of the nation's leading regional botanical gardens.

The conservatory's initial design emphasized the appearance of its elements as separate underground structures.

Sunrise at the conservatory.

The search for an architect had several false starts before one was found who would put the garden on the architectural and botanical map. In December 1981 the search committee picked architect Carl Groos, a noted San Antonio native practicing in Denver, but he died suddenly. Next chosen was E. Fay Jones, one of the last surviving associates of Frank Lloyd Wright, but he withdrew citing a health problem. Finally, in April 1982, the committee selected Emilio Ambasz, a promising forty-year-old architect born in Argentina.[2]

After graduating from Princeton University, Ambasz had helped establish the Institute for Architecture and Urban Studies in New York and served as curator of design at New York's Museum of Modern Art from 1969 to 1976. He left to establish his own firm, began work in industrial and mechanical design, and opened offices in New York and Italy. But in 1982 his growing reputation for imaginative architecture was still based on unbuilt projects notable for introducing landscape as an architectural element.[3]

The great botanical conservatories of the nineteenth century, from London and Edinburgh to Philadelphia, New York, Pittsburgh, and Washington, DC, were soaring glass enclosures designed to let in as much sunlight as possible and keep out rain, wind, and snow. A conservatory in the southwestern United States needed instead to reduce and regulate the intense summer sunlight and fierce temperatures, which could exceed 100 degrees for days on end. By the 1980s, newly developed systems for monitoring temperature, light, and humidity were contributing to a burst of new conservatories being built in warmer climates, including ones in Atlanta, Oklahoma City, and San Antonio.

To deal with San Antonio's particularly oppressive South Texas climate, Ambasz's design took advantage of the insulating qualities of the soil. Rather than a single large structure enclosed in glass, Ambasz designed one broken into separate units, each with berms of earth around its base that would reduce utility costs by 20 percent. More than 1,200 panes held in place by aluminum frames formed conical or pyramidal "glass hats" positioned to take advantage of exposure to the sun and wind flow.[4]

Computers at San Antonio's conservatory were designed to adjust the intensity of interior light by raising or lowering twenty-one thousand square feet of indoor mesh sunshades, later abandoned, covering the angled inside glass surfaces, a system used notably in the Rockefeller Wing of the Metropolitan Museum of Art. Underground turbines controlling airflow through wall vents could change the air every three minutes, maintaining a temperature of 85 degrees even when it was 100 outside. A permanent shade covering the west glass wall reduced heat and light on hot afternoons.

Ambasz's design for what was later named the Lucile Halsell Conservatory won a major prize—the Progressive Architecture Award—in early 1985, months before ground was even broken, validating at the outset his creative approach to a modern conservatory resistant to hot weather.

In mid-May 1982 the city had approved the project, with the expected caveats that the botanical society would bear all architectural, engineering, and construction costs, and that the building, when complete, would become property of the city, which owned the land. New botanical garden director Eric Tschanz characterized the site as having "some of the worst soil in San Antonio." In wet weather it could shift six or seven inches, requiring massive concrete substructures that, with the berms, would make the conservatory seem to have been built underground.[5]

Conservatory architect Emilio Ambasz (*left*) visits at the construction site with Hall Hammond, the botanical society's first president.

Denman spent a day in New York with Ambasz in October 1982 discussing site plans and design concepts. Ambasz next came to San Antonio to inspect the site with Denman and Hall Hammond, the San Antonio Botanical Society's first president. Bruce McAlpin of the New York Botanical Garden was hired as a horticultural consultant for the design. Chumney, Jones and Kell—later JonesKell—was chosen as the local associated architect.[6]

The city was as happy to have someone else doing the project as Denman and botanical society leaders were to have the independence to do it. By relying solely on the Ewing Halsell Foundation and private donors for funds, the conservatory could be completed using materials and professionals of Denman's and the society's choosing, free of requirements to accept lowest bids.[7]

The steel tempietto on an overlook above the conservatory provides a view of San Antonio's skyline.

The foundation made building the conservatory its "most ambitious project ever to be undertaken" to date, contributing some 90 percent of the $6.9 million cost that today would exceed $26 million. Even so, the botanical society faced limitations. By early 1984 cost estimates exceeded the budget by more than $1 million despite the architect's efforts to reduce overruns. That led to elimination of one of the three pyramidal rooms planned on the southern perimeter, over the architect's protest that "from a design point of view the composition exists much better with three elements along the Funston Street side." That room was to have been devoted to succulents, but what were later named the Kleberg Desert Pavilion and the Gretchen Northrup Tropical Pavilion remained. Another victim of cost-cutting was the level of the conservatory courtyard, which was intended to be five feet deeper.[8]

Cost issues also delayed construction of a steel tempietto, a small temple-like pavilion to replace the 1980 wooden gazebo atop the overlook north of the conservatory. The tempietto was later built in the style of the conservatory, and the gazebo was moved to become the focal point of what is now the Rare and Endangered Garden.[9]

Botanical garden supervisor Paul Cox stands beside workers unloading a tree acquired on a collecting trip to Florida in 1984.

Plant collection for the conservatory began in summer 1984, before construction started. Some plants were donated by friends, others by fellow institutions like the Honolulu Botanical Gardens and the Marie Selby Botanical Gardens in Sarasota, Florida. But most were found in small specialty nurseries or backyard greenhouses of rare plant collectors. Director Eric Tshanz sent a pair of horticulturists—botanical garden supervisor Paul Cox and Steve Gaydos—on six buying trips that became adventures.[10]

"Obtaining the plants was a task equal to the scope of the conservatory project," Cox said. On their first trip the two flew to Florida and rented a truck to fill and drive back. Faced with a limited acquisition budget, they developed "scrounging techniques," which Cox defined as acquiring "plant material without theft or deception but also without paying money for it." They did this by exploiting "a professional courtesy that exists among plant enthusiasts"—that is, giving surplus plants to fellow enthusiasts.

The two had opposite methods. "If I saw something that struck my fancy and they didn't offer it right away," Cox said, "I would look transfixed at the plant with a wistful expression until the host would say, 'Like to have one of those?'"

Gaydos took a more aggressive approach, Cox recalled. "He would pick up a plant, eye it hungrily while turning it around in his hands, and say, 'This is nice, can I have one?'" The pair drove the truck home "filled to capacity, with leaves sticking out from under the back door."

Next they flew to Arizona to collect Sonoran Desert plants. "After scrounging a pretty good load from the Phoenix area," Cox said, they drove their rented truck to Tucson, where the state agriculture department had permission to donate three giant saguaro cacti in the path of bulldozers. Loading the three, which stood up to thirteen feet tall, was "uneventful."

A few months later the horticulturists heard of a nursery closing in San Juan Capistrano, California. The two "descended like vultures" and made "some phenomenal buys" of palm species that were under quarantine in Florida and the Rio Grande Valley but could be obtained safely in California. Particular prizes were *Licuala spinosa* palms, which they bought for a fraction

Three giant saguaro cacti in Arizona were uprooted, lowered on a pneumatic support, and hoisted into crates for transport to the botanical garden.

of their value. Across town in the California community they found higher prices but still outstanding specimens.

On their last trip to Florida, Cox and Gaydos visited twenty-four nurseries in a four-day span, returning with more than 250 tropical species in a truck "so full we had to push the doors back with a loader so they could be locked." The two lost no plants on the journey nor while unloading them in San Antonio for storage in greenhouses and in a temporary structure for larger specimens until the conservatory was ready.[11]

After more than three years of planning, groundbreaking ceremonies for the conservatory were held in August 1985. Guido Brothers Construction Company excavated for several weeks before foundations were poured.[12]

As the conservatory neared completion two years later, leading architectural critics feasted on its unique features. Of the conservatory's ninety thousand square feet, more than 80 percent were open. The 20 percent under glass roofs were divided among six separate climate-controlled viewing areas surrounded by earthen berms sixteen to twenty-five feet tall. From a distance the conservatory's profile was uncluttered, revealing only glass rooflines above what appeared to be a meadow spreading over some three acres. But Paul Goldberger wrote in the *New York Times* that "the underground quality is an illusion," as the completed conservatory complex stood at ground level, with soil "bermed up around it to heighten the sense of connection to the earth."[13]

A small passage that to Goldberger seemed to be "burrowing through the earth like a tunnel" served as the main entrance to the conservatory complex. First came a small circular entrance room with an open roof where buried refrigeration coils cooled a small alpine garden hermetically sealed in one wall, a display eventually abandoned when consistently low temperatures could not be maintained.

CACTI ANATOMY
ANATOMÍA DEL CACTO

Among the conservatory's key elements are the palm room, desert room, tropical room, fern room, and a seasonal exhibition room.

The passage then opened to a large circular seasonal exhibition room with a conical glass roof. What appeared to be a canopy tree in the center was an eighteen-foot-tall frame of welded steel pipe covered by cork bark providing a base for cascading epiphytes—mosses, orchids, and bromeliads. Past the exhibition room came a trapezoidal courtyard with a pool of lily pads and lotus, a panoramic view of support columns, and, Goldberger noted, "a set of conical and angular structures poking up out of the earth like huge abstract sculptures of glass and steel."

Two pavilions topped by glass pyramids and with appropriate temperature and humidity settings opened from the courtyard's southern side: a desert room and a hot tropical conservatory with lush equatorial plants and exotic blossoms.[14]

On the courtyard's northern side was an orangery, its fruit trees set in massive planters of volcanic stone, later removed. The orangery opened into a fern room with walls and ledges of simulated rock and a flat roof of paned glass. The tropical grotto of ferns, orchids, and cacti with a waterfall and a lily pond, which survives, was kept humid by continuous misting that kept the temperature below 80 degrees.

From its main entry the courtyard narrowed to a focal point: the Palm House, a 110-foot cone, three-quarters of its circumference enclosed in glass and the rest left open. A 100-foot double coconut palm from the Seychelles became the centerpiece of one of the nation's leading collections of palms and cycads that followed a perimeter walkway spiraling up to a roof deck. A 75-foot coconut palm and 40-foot betel nut palm stood nearby.

On June 15, 1987, the Ewing Halsell Foundation sponsored a two-day early dedication of the conservatory, by then 90 percent complete. It began with a symposium, Glass Houses for People and for Plants, moderated by *Dallas Morning News* architecture critic David Dillon at the St. Anthony Hotel.

Excavation for conservatory construction began in August 1985.

A late afternoon tour of the unfinished conservatory was followed by a ceremony at Trinity University's Margarite B. Parker Chapel, where botanical society president Helen Hogan symbolically presented the conservatory as a gift to the city of San Antonio. It was accepted by Mayor Pro Tem Jimmy Hasslocher. A San Antonio Symphony concert in the chapel came next, beginning with Beethoven's overture *The Consecration of the House*. The concert was a scheduled event of that year's weeklong San Antonio Festival, a short-lived annual arts fiesta begun by Gilbert Denman.

The next morning Richard A. Howard, director of the Arnold Arboretum of Harvard University, chaired the session "Botanical Gardens and the Crises of Species Extinction," held at Trinity University.[15]

A more traditional event came eight months later, on the afternoon of Sunday, February 28, 1988, when the completed Lucile Halsell Conservatory opened to a crowd of more than fourteen thousand. City councilman Weir Labatt and botanical society president Pat Deely cut the ceremonial ribbon. Those present were appropriately awed by Ambasz's first major building, which *New Republic* architecture critic Herbert Muschamp termed "a milestone in contemporary architecture."[16]

Guests dined at the conservatory the night before its formal opening on February 28, 1988, when more than fourteen thousand San Antonians lined up to enter.

Paul Goldberger observed in the *New York Times* that Ambasz took "a particular joy in rethinking common, everyday situations." The Lucile Halsell Conservatory, "his most ambitious such rethinking," he wrote, "is unlike any conservatory ever built."[17]

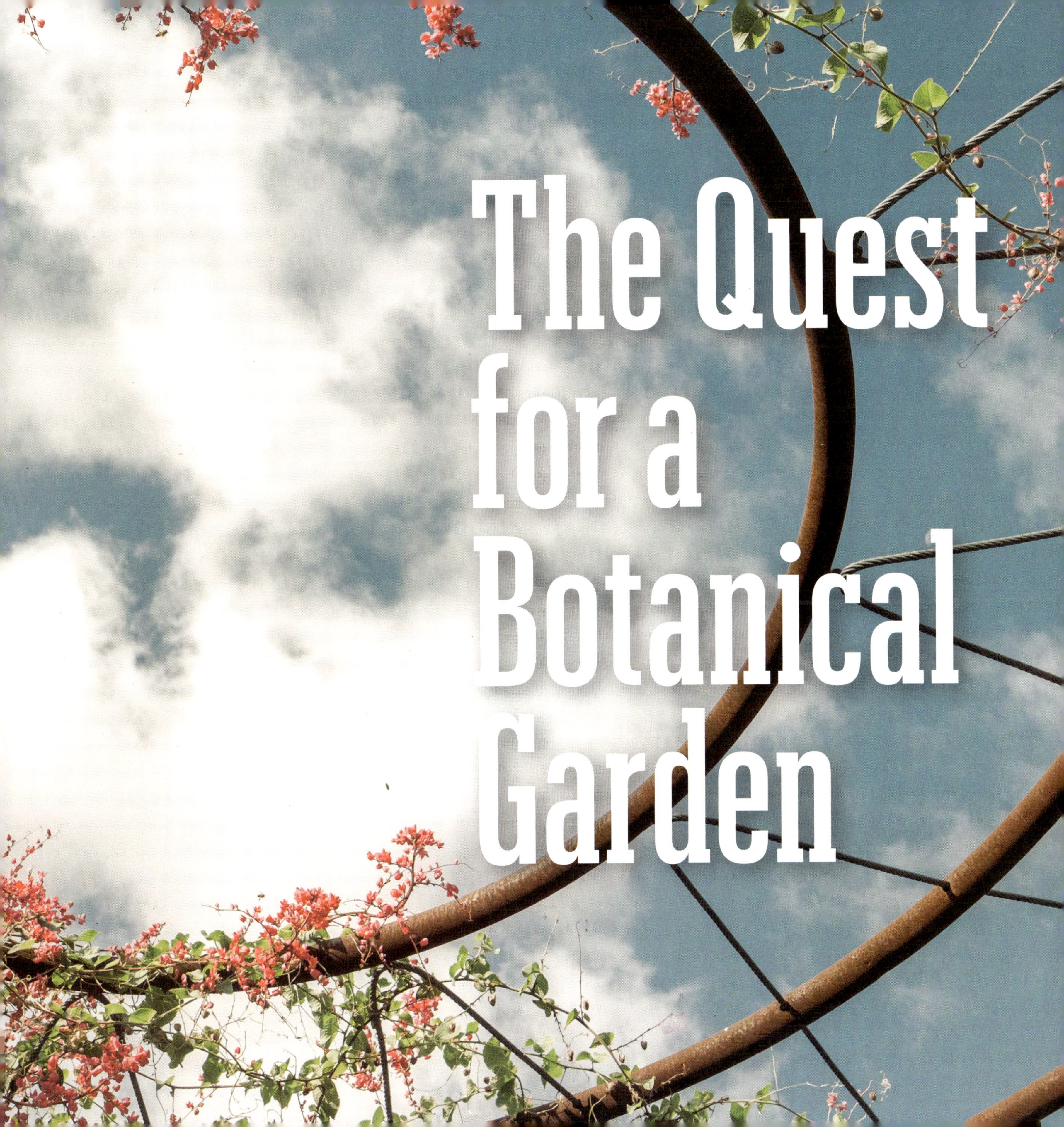

The Quest for a Botanical Garden

Clouds are framed by the trellis atop the Family Adventure Garden's Semmes Prickly Pear Peak.

A Dozen Tries since 1884

San Antonio eked out its existence on the edge of the frontier until 1877, when rail travel replaced stagecoaches, oxcarts, and horseback as the only way to get in or out. In the city's rush to catch up with basic elements of more civilized places, few amenities seemed less worthy of its to-do list than a botanical garden.

But only seven years later, in March 1884, an obscure investor named M. C. Henry made what appears to be the first proposal for a botanical garden in San Antonio. He asked the city council for a ground lease to establish a garden near the city cemeteries in the eastern part of town. His request was referred to the Committee on Public Improvements, but nothing was heard back.[18]

The idea resurfaced just a year later. The new Museum of Natural History in San Pedro Springs Park planned a zoological garden, which soon opened, and a botanical garden "for rare trees, shrubs, and plants," which did not.[19]

For nearly another century more propositions advanced a range of parks, quarries, and creek sides for a garden until one group solved the puzzle of how and where to create, at last, a major botanical garden for the city.

Proposals for botanical gardens early in San Antonio's post-1877 transformation parallel aspirations in Renaissance Europe, where modern botanical gardens originated. Eight survive from sixteenth-century Europe, most at universities. First was the University of Pisa's, established in 1543 as a research facility for botanist Luca Ghini. It moved from the banks of the Arno River to higher ground in 1563, forfeiting the title of world's oldest botanical garden to the University of Padua's garden, which has stayed put, on the same five and a half acres, since it was created by the senate of the Venetian Republic in 1545 to help students distinguish genuine medicinal plants from false ones.[20]

The oldest surviving botanical garden in the United States is Philadelphia's 45-acre Bartram's Garden, begun in 1728. Today's United States Botanic Garden opened in

Washington, DC, in 1850. In Saint Louis the 79-acre Missouri Botanical Garden began in 1859 and has the nation's oldest continuously operating greenhouse, dating to 1882. The 250-acre New York Botanical Garden opened in 1891.

Being a large city, however, did not guarantee ease in establishing a botanical garden. San Francisco, for one, with more economic and geographical advantages than San Antonio, developed plans for a garden in the 1880s but gained no funding until 1927. It took another thirteen years before what is today the San Francisco Botanical Garden at Strybing Arboretum opened on fifty-five acres in Golden Gate Park.

Residential landscaping had become competitive in San Antonio by 1910 as calls increased for a municipal botanical garden.

San Antonians were using the term "botanical garden" loosely. Did they mean a study garden for a particular type of plant, like those with medical uses in early European botanical gardens? Was theirs meant to gather unfamiliar varieties for scientific study, like botanist and horticulturist John Bartram's pioneering garden in Philadelphia? To protect and conserve plants on the order of the Missouri Botanical Garden in Saint Louis? Or simply to provide an entertaining display of flowering plants and shrubs from here and there like Tampa Bay's Busch Gardens, with its tropical rainforest named Jungala across from a ride through the Congo River Rapids?

Indeed, just which "famous gardens in other American cities" San Antonians planned to emulate was not clear as their suggestions accelerated early in the twentieth century. Including the term "botanical," though, does suggest a desire to be more than just a floral garden, a feature gaining popularity in landscaping of the city's public parks and private homes. In 1911 George Washington Brackenridge proposed a "unique and beautiful" botanical garden on fifteen miles of unusable floodplain a quarter of a mile wide along Salado Creek north of Fort Sam Houston. He promised to provide backup water by drilling a new artesian well if the fifty or so farmers along the strip would donate the land. They would not.[21]

Three years later a legislative committee brought up Brackenridge Park as a potential site for a state botanical garden displaying the ornamental and fruit-bearing trees and shrubs of Texas. One advocate thought "Texans have spent too much of their time trying to cultivate trees and shrubs of the Atlantic seaboard, which cannot grow in this climate and which are not superior, even if equal, to our native plants."[22]

Then municipal plans arose for the former rock quarry west of Brackenridge Park as the site of the Pan-American Exposition, a world's fair to celebrate San Antonio's bicentennial in 1918. There would be four permanent buildings—an auditorium, art gallery, historical museum, and a building for a botanical garden. In January 1916 a Texas delegation of fifteen

San Antonians, headed by U.S. senator Morris Sheppard, met in Washington, DC, with President Woodrow Wilson and cabinet members and received pledges of support. Such assurances did not suffice, however, to gain passage of a city bond issue for funding. Hampered by the onset of World War I, exposition plans went no further.[23]

By then a new parks commissioner, Ray Lambert, had begun his signature project in Brackenridge Park—the transformation of a former quarry pit into a Japanese Tea Garden "modeled somewhat" on the one in San Francisco's Golden Gate Park. Another inspiration came from Busch Gardens in Pasadena, California. Lambert thought Busch Gardens was a fine model for a botanical garden adjacent to Brackenridge on the ten acres of former poor farm fields donated by Bexar County as Davis Park. He realized that brewer Adolphus Busch "was not forced to curtail his expenses, as we would be compelled to do," but using city prisoners to prepare the grounds for gardeners already at work in the park could result in "a botanical garden the equal of any in the country."[24]

W. S. Delery, the assistant city engineer, drew up plans for the garden. In 1917 Lambert announced that soft shell pecans and magnolia trees would be planted first, followed by palm seedlings. A serious botanical aspect was indicated during a visit to Washington by Lambert and city engineer Hans Helland, who were encouraged in their efforts by the president of the American Horticultural Association. Lambert and Helland also visited the United States Botanic Garden, whose officials promised donation of rare plants.[25]

Lambert promoted this support, though the *San Antonio Light* feared that his plans had "been handicapped for lack of a modern hothouse or conservatory." In 1919 *San Antonio Evening News* columnist Marin B. Fenwick swung in to endorse the project, writing that "nothing adds a greater attraction to a city than a fine botanical garden." She praised the planned display of plants, flowers, and trees from throughout Texas but noted candidly, "It is one of the calamities that nothing can be done without money, and as yet none of the oil magnates are in San Antonio." Sure enough, little backing was found, and no botanical garden materialized.[26]

A successor for Brackenridge Park's floral Texas star, shown before being replaced by the Sunken Garden Theater, was planned in Mahncke Park, designated by the city in 1934 as a botanical garden.

In 1929 the *Light* proposed a wildflower preserve as a botanical garden, which it editorialized would be a good use for the flood plain upstream from the new Olmos Dam. Four years later the city came up with the idea of a botanical garden in a pit in the old quarries west of Brackenridge Park. This time the quarries were to be transformed not for a Pan-American Exposition, as in 1918, but as San Jacinto Park, San Antonio's entry for the site of the Texas Centennial Exposition of 1936. The proposition was nixed when the exposition went to Dallas.[27]

At this point San Antonio's Business and Professional Women's Club proposed a botanical garden in the oddly configured and perennially neglected Mahncke Park (pronounced MANK-ee), between Brackenridge Park and Fort Sam Houston. The group proposed that it would help the city manage a garden there "similar to famous gardens in other American cities." In June 1934 the city adopted an ordinance approving the club's plan and designating the park as a botanical garden, to start with a 122-by-150-foot plot on Funston Place near Broadway. Plants from throughout the state would encircle a grouping of bluebonnets, phlox, verbena, and rock daisies to form a Texas star, blooming in succession so that state colors could be seen throughout the summer. This would replace the popular floral star recently removed to make way for Brackenridge Park's Sunken Garden Theater and would be ready in time for the Texas centennial in 1936.[28]

In June 1935 the city announced completion of plans and said plantings would begin "within a few days." The next spring a *San Antonio Express* report hedged that the effort "though well advanced was necessarily a labor of years." Little more was heard of the garden, for this was in the depths of the Depression, and the beleaguered professional women's club had to maintain its loan fund for struggling businesswomen and build its scholarship fund.[29]

Gender dynamics may also have hindered progress between the city and the club. Its members challenged contemporary social norms not just by working outside the home but by referring to themselves by other than their husbands' names. One of the club's botanical garden committee members, the wife of florist Fred Huffmeyer, identified herself in the newspaper not as Mrs. Fred Huffmeyer but as Mrs. Nora Huffmeyer. Other married club members did the same, to the probable discomfort of the staid establishment.[30]

A group of more traditional women—one whose members did not typically work outside the home and who, among other conformities, subordinated their public identities to those of their husbands—was able to take a botanical garden across the finish line. These ladies organized the San Antonio Garden Center, which later sponsored establishment of the San Antonio Botanical Garden. To this day the two organizers of the garden center have been universally referred to only as Mrs. Robert R. Witt, whose husband owned a building supply company, and Mrs. Joseph R. Murphy, whose husband was vice president of the same company. They and others are liberated from such identities in this book.

Harriet Witt and Lucretia Murphy were early members of a garden club formed by the Junior League of San Antonio in March 1931 as an affiliate of the Garden Club of America. The San Antonio Garden Club sought to expand its civic beautification efforts by encouraging interest in gardening and nurtured offshoot clubs that held monthly meetings in their neighborhoods and annual joint meetings at the Junior League's headquarters, the Bright Shawl building on Augusta Street. Fledgling subsidiaries became independent clubs and numbered at least eight by 1940.[31]

Under Harriet Witt and Lucretia Murphy's leadership, the clubs joined together as a federation, the San Antonio Garden Center, in February 1940. The center first met on a Witte Museum patio in front of the Hand Weavers House, a night watchman's quarters converted to house the looms of craftworkers' Hand Weavers Guild. The garden center initially focused on promoting information and plant exchanges on the patio—potted specimens sold for one cent each—on Wednesdays, free admission day at the Witte. Presiding over the morning exchanges was Harriet Witt, the center's first president; afternoons were overseen by Lucretia Murphy, who became the center's second president.[32]

By 1942 the garden center had grown to a federation of seventeen clubs, and its meetings were moved to the first floor of the newly restored Twohig house along the river

Fundraising efforts that eventually targeted the botanical garden were undertaken in 1933 by San Antonio Garden Club members (*from left*) Ollie Rogers, Marguerite Hall, Ethel Brough, and Holland Woodhull for the club's second fall flower show at the Witte Museum.

behind the Witte Museum. Ten years later the number of clubs had doubled and included the Men's Garden Club. Meetings moved into the Witte's newly completed Memorial Auditorium, built in part with garden center flower show proceeds donated for its construction. Profits were next redirected to another cause—the garden center's own fund for building a permanent home.[33]

Memorial Auditorium's seating capacity was 250, but in the 1950s the garden center's number of affiliated clubs surpassed eighty and their combined membership exceeded three thousand. One lecture-demonstration—on the religious symbolism of flowers by a Michigan State horticulture professor—was so crowded that it had to be repeated twice. In addition to a larger auditorium, the center needed classrooms, a conservation center, experimental plant growing rooms, and a reference library.[34]

In November 1954 the center held its first event officially benefiting a fund for its own building—the event was a modest presentation by the Broadway Flower Shop about Christmas decorations. The next month came the center's second annual Christmas home pilgrimage, one of two major annual fundraising projects. The other was a spring flower show that in 1955 morphed into a three-day extravaganza at Freeman Coliseum drawing some twenty thousand viewers.[35]

Although some latter-day accounts assert—without documentation—that establishing a botanical garden was a founding goal of the San Antonio Garden Center in 1940, none of the many newspaper accounts that can be found dealing with the center's history and goals mentions a botanical garden until 1956, when the center began serious negotiations for a headquarters location. Even then a botanical garden was lumped in with "other facilities" that the new space could accommodate.[36]

That left room for sporadic suggestions like one from the city's Parks and Recreation Department director in 1952. At San Pedro Springs Park, where declining artesian water pressure had sapped the park's fabled springs and water-starved heritage oaks were dying, the director proposed sealing off half of the park's new swimming pool, planting water lilies in the other half and stocking it with fish, and calling it a botanical garden. But he was one of five directors who ran the department in the politically chaotic five years following adoption of a new city charter, and his successors all ignored the idea.[37]

In September 1956 the city council agreed to consider the garden center's request to build its headquarters in the upper portion of Mahncke Park, on the east side of North New Braunfels Avenue. "It's not costing us anything," parks director Robert Fraser said. "Eventually they'll put as much as $500,000 into the project." The city, however, soon indicated that it would neither contribute to the center's construction nor grant a lease for longer than twenty-five years, and the center lost interest in the location.[38]

In February 1960 the center accepted a gift of seven acres from Lee R. and Bessie Pletz for a headquarters and botanical garden on Vance Jackson Road, north of what would become Loop 410, as an amenity of the Colonial Hills subdivision they were developing. The donation required construction to begin within five years. But after three years passed with no work started, the center, then led by Amelia Thacker, had second thoughts and in November 1962 renewed its request to the city council for a building site in Mahncke Park. Two months later the council gave the center a year to provide a building proposal for its consideration.[39]

In the meantime another alternative emerged. O'Neil Ford, the coordinating architect for HemisFair, the 1968 world's fair being planned for downtown, suggested that the garden center sponsor a permanent, large, enclosed, temperature-controlled botanical garden on the fairgrounds "in which plants from throughout the world could be grown year-round." A nearby building would house the center's offices, meeting rooms, and library. A group from the center met with Ford and Ewen Dingwall, the fair's executive vice president, in July 1964, and decided to go forward if the city council rejected the second Mahncke Park proposal.[40]

Then the garden center's fortunes changed dramatically.

In May 1963 Lila Cockrell, an advocate for the parks, took office as San Antonio's first woman elected to the city council. She sympathized with garden center president Dorothy Colemere's presentation of the center's proposal. In October 1964 the council approved the center's plans to fund and construct a headquarters building costing nearly $150,000, more than $1.1 million in today's dollars. The center hoped the city would contribute to construction. The council named Cockrell as its representative to negotiate terms. She worked with the cochairs of the center's building committee, Louise Briggs and Irene Turner.[41]

The new councilwoman and center leaders apparently hit it off, for two months later Cockrell's house was one of seven on

Completion of the garden center building in Mahncke Park in 1966 shifted members' attention to a botanical garden.

the center's annual Christmas pilgrimage of homes. Cockrell soon took the lead in blocking a U.S. Army request to extend Parland Place east to Austin Road, later known as Old Austin Road, to give Fort Sam Houston traffic a direct link to Broadway. This would have cut through the proposed garden center area and bisected the heart of the unpromising site above it.[42]

By mid-1965 there was a deal. The city would not pay any building construction costs but would agree to fund a 144-car parking lot and maintain the building, which would, after all, be on city property and be owned by the city. The center pared back building costs by nearly 40 percent to $90,000, closer to the amount in its building fund. The city balked at being liable for damage claims, but the issue went away when the center agreed to carry sufficient insurance.[43]

In October 1966 the center dedicated its headquarters, a one-story, 5,250-square-foot red brick structure with cedar shake shingles and a commanding view of the San Antonio River Valley west across North New Braunfels Avenue. As a mark of gratitude, Councilwoman Cockrell was named an honorary life member.[44]

One celebratory newspaper article took twenty column inches to list civic beautification projects the center had been involved in through the years. The headline of a much smaller story announced: "Botanical Garden to be Added Attraction."[45]

San Antonio's restored 1878 reservoir hosted a summertime Shakespeare in the Park performance.

A Reservoir in Washington Heights

Up the slope from the new San Antonio Garden Center headquarters, a large depression encircled the remains of a stone reservoir, with little hint of its importance in helping turn San Antonio into a modern city. Converted into an amphitheater, it became a singular historic landmark for the San Antonio Botanical Garden.

The reservoir's origin, use, and abandonment parallel the decades of change and growth of the city it helped create. It had been the focal point of the four acres purchased by the San Antonio Water Works Company in 1877 as the site of a reservoir to store and supply water for the city's new water system. It was incorporated into the San Antonio Botanical Garden—along with twenty-five adjoining acres that have their own backstory as part of a major suburban tract once named Washington Heights.

San Antonio stood as an isolated outpost on the Texas frontier for more than a century and a half, its seclusion finally broken when the railroad arrived in February 1877, kicking off a spurt of civic progress that included replacing the Spanish-era, gravity-driven acequias, or ditches, that flowed only downward and could not reach development expanding up even slight slopes.

To build that new water system, the city—two months after rail service began—picked the newly formed San Antonio Water Works Company, headed by Jean Batiste LaCoste, a French immigrant, merchant, ice manufacturer, and major stockholder in the company.

LaCoste started at a secluded spot on the San Antonio River at the northern edge of today's Brackenridge Park, where he had a short raceway dug to a new two-level stone pumphouse. There he installed two water-driven turbines, which

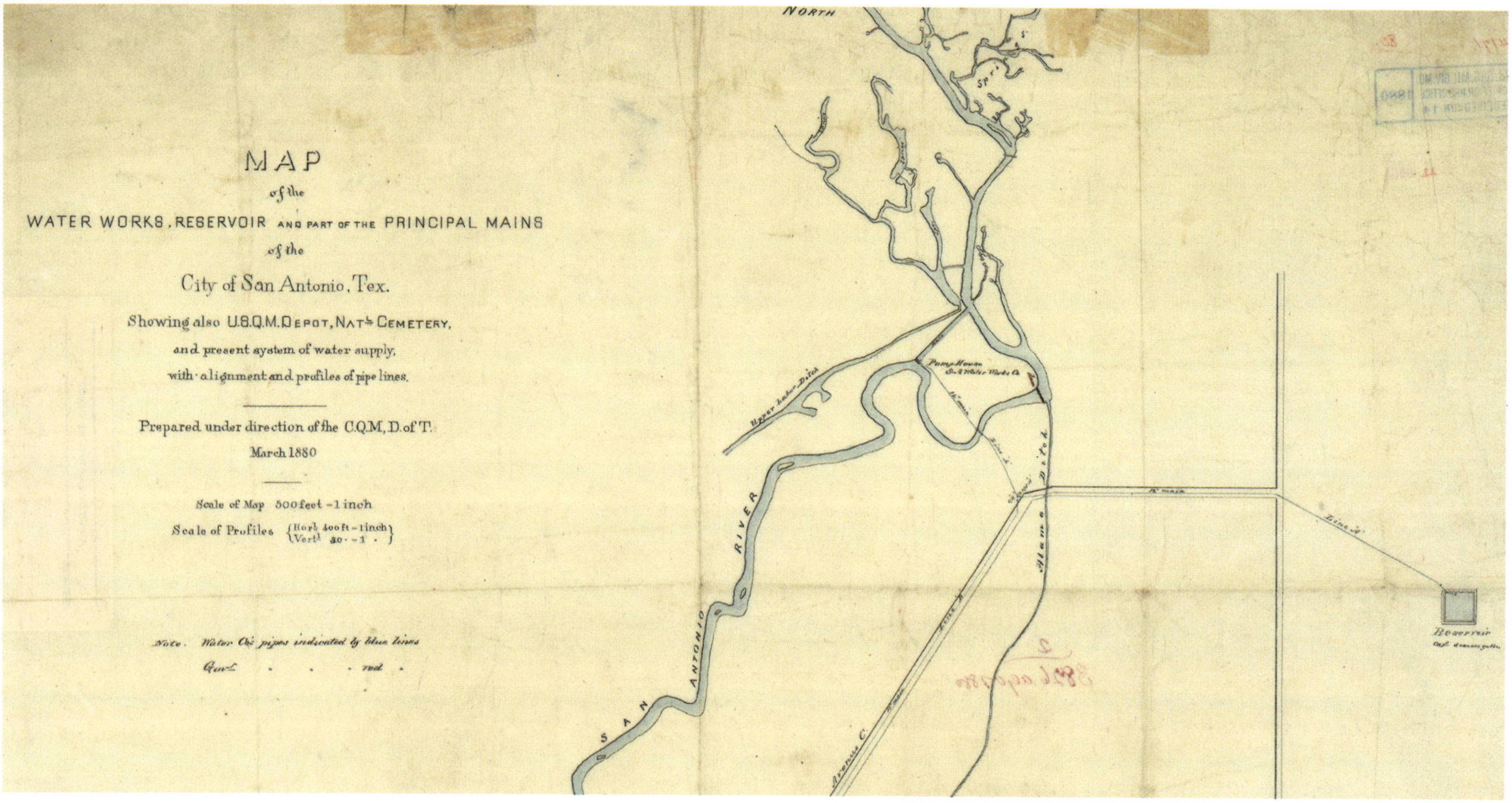

Army engineers outlined the source of water for San Antonio's first modern water system in this detail of an 1880 map. A pumphouse (*center right*), now in Brackenridge Park, sent river water up present-day Pershing Avenue to fill a stone reservoir (*far right*), now an amphitheater in the botanical garden.

arrived quickly by rail from the contractor, King Iron Bridge & Manufacturing Company of Cleveland, Ohio, and not after days aboard ox-driven wagons bumping along rutted roads from a coastal port, as had been necessary only months before. The turbines could force as much as 1.25 million gallons a day of river water underground up to a new reservoir.[46]

Initially the Water Works Company planned for the reservoir to be built "on the upper part of the rock quarries," near where a water tower now stands by the intersection of Hildebrand Avenue and Devine Road. But plans changed, and the company relocated the reservoir to a site northeast of the center of town, along the road to Austin and atop a ridge that marks the start of the foothills rising slowly from the coastal plain to form the Texas Hill Country. There the water company bought four acres for the reservoir from French-born businessman François Guilbeau Jr., who also served as French consul. Financier George Brackenridge, the closest San Antonio got to a stereotypical late-nineteenth-century tycoon, would purchase a thousand surrounding acres as an investment.[47]

The task of building a stone reservoir fell to subcontractor Thomas Cavanaugh. It was no small task. The reservoir was reported to be 213 feet square and 20 twenty feet deep, surrounded by 6-foot gravel embankments, and able to hold five million gallons of water.[48]

Cavanaugh began work with a "full force of men and mules with plows, scrapers, picks, and shovels" digging into the caliche and throwing it up around the perimeter, where

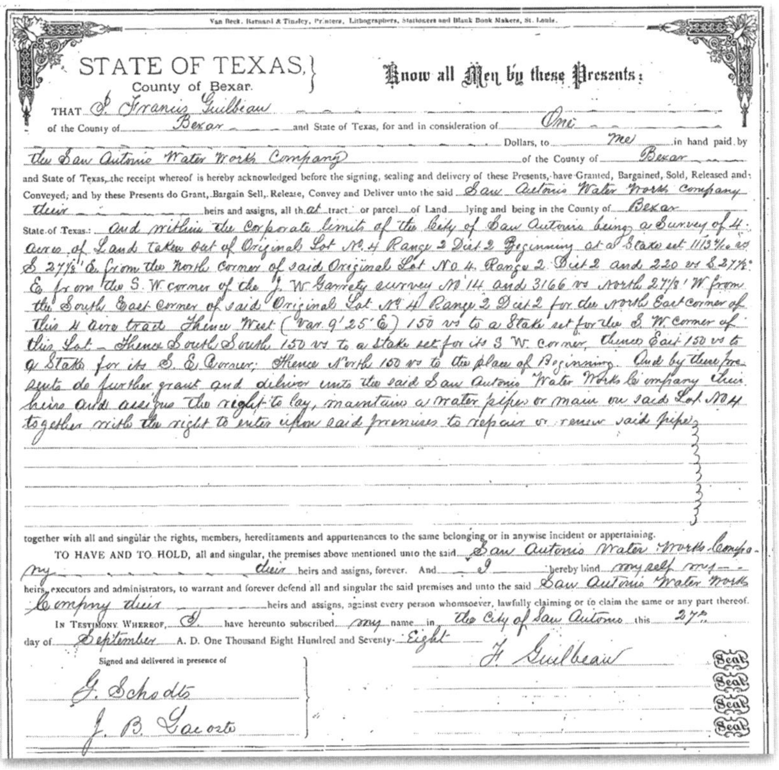

Van Beck, Barnard & Tinsley, Printers, Lithographers, Stationers and Blank Book Makers, St. Louis.

STATE OF TEXAS, County of Bexar. }

Know all Men by these Presents:

THAT J. Francis Guilbeau of the County of Bexar and State of Texas, for and in consideration of One Dollars, to me in hand paid by the San Antonio Water Works Company of the County of Bexar and State of Texas, the receipt whereof is hereby acknowledged before the signing, sealing and delivery of these Presents, have Granted, Bargained, Sold, Released and Conveyed; and by these Presents do Grant, Bargain Sell, Release, Convey and Deliver unto the said San Antonio Water Works company their heirs and assigns, all that tract or parcel of Land lying and being in the County of Bexar State of Texas: And within the Corporate limits of the City of San Antonio being a Survey of 4 acres of Land taken out of Original Lot No. 4 Range 2 Dist 2 Beginning at a Stake set 1113⅞ vs S 27½° E from the North Corner of said Original Lot No 4 Range 2 Dist 2 and 220 vs S 27½° E from the S. W. corner of the J. W. Garrety survey No 14 and 3166 vs North 27½' W from the South East corner of said Original Lot No 4 Range 2 Dist 2 for the North East corner of this 4 acre tract Thence West (Var. 9'25'E) 150 vs to a Stake set for the S. W. corner of this Lot – Thence South South 150 vs to a stake set for its S W. corner, thence East 150 vs to a Stake for its S. E. Corner; Thence North 150 vs to the place of Beginning. And by these presents do further grant and deliver unto the said San Antonio Water Works Company their heirs and assigns the right to lay, maintain a water pipe or main on said Lot No 4 together with the right to enter upon said premises to repair or renew said pipe

together with all and singular the rights, members, hereditaments and appurtenances to the same belonging or in anywise incident or appertaining.

TO HAVE AND TO HOLD, all and singular, the premises above mentioned unto the said San Antonio Water Works Company their heirs and assigns, forever. And I hereby bind myself my heirs, executors and administrators, to warrant and forever defend all and singular the said premises and unto the said San Antonio Water Works Company their heirs and assigns, against every person whomsoever, lawfully claiming or to claim the same or any part thereof.

IN TESTIMONY WHEREOF, I have hereunto subscribed my name in the City of San Antonio this 27th day of September A. D. One Thousand Eight Hundred and Seventy-Eight

F. Guilbeau [Seal]

Signed and delivered in presence of

G. Schodts

J. B. Lacoste

In 1878 Water Works president Jean LaCoste (*seated*) purchased four acres for his company's reservoir from François Guilbeau Jr., who also served as French consul in San Antonio.

Financier George Brackenridge took over the debt-ridden San Antonio Water Works Company in 1883.

it formed an impervious lining for walls of limestone blocks hauled up from city quarries near the river. Builders included stone pillars inside the reservoir to support a stone roof in case it was desired later, which it was not. Since the pumphouse began operating in July 1878, before the reservoir was finished, the pumps initially sent water directly into city pipes without benefit of a reservoir to hold a backup supply.[49]

In March 1879 Cavanaugh advertised for twenty stone masons to wrap up construction, enabling him to finish four weeks later. Filling the reservoir took three days, since some water had to be retained in the river to supply the acequia system, kept in parallel use for two more decades. Some fluffing made the desolate area more appealing for an afternoon carriage drive. The *San Antonio Express* noted, with no elaboration, that "Mr. LaCoste and Mr. Brackenridge have put their wits together to render its surroundings attractive." Water Works president Jean LaCoste invited city officials to an evening reservoir viewing reception on April 7, 1879. They pronounced themselves well pleased.[50]

Completion of the water system, however, did not guarantee smooth times for the San Antonio Water Works. Initial demand for its water did not meet expectations. Tightfisted San Antonians wondered why they should pay for water when it still flowed free past their homes in acequias. If they wanted cleaner water, they could buy it from passing vendors who illegally filled their tanks with reservoir water from fire hydrants. The beleaguered LaCoste used Water Works stock as collateral for loans from Brackenridge's bank, and when he could not pay, Brackenridge soon owned the majority of the stock and became president of the company. By 1883, along with a few friends and relatives, he owned all of the stock and LaCoste was out.[51]

One of Brackenridge's first challenges was dealing with charges that water in the unroofed reservoir was contaminated. From the outset it had been stocked with French carp, counted upon to skim impurities from standing water. But some users complained that they found dead fish, eels, and even snakes from the reservoir in downtown pipes, and therefore the reservoir's water was polluted.[52]

Brackenridge retorted with a strong defense. There could be no pure water without fish, he declared, but strainers at the mouth of the main outlet pipe were so rigorously maintained that fish two inches long could not enter the pipes, much less snakes or eels, and the water delivered was as pure as water could be. "If those who claim to have seen so many snakes would drink more of the water and less of something stronger," he said, "they would see fewer snakes and enjoy better health."[53]

Increasing awareness of the importance of sanitation brought fears that accumulation of dead birds and unhealthy detritus in the open water supply risked a return of diphtheria or typhoid epidemics. Foreboding was compounded by reports that soldiers from nearby Fort Sam Houston bathed in the reservoir, despite the prohibition of such activity in an 1885 city ordinance. Even though there was a cottage nearby for a watchman, offenses continued. A hunter was caught shooting ducks and wading into the reservoir's stepped-down interior to retrieve them.[54]

Solutions to some matters required improvisation. During fires in the city, Water Works engineer Herman Dittmar stationed himself near the pumphouse and focused a telescope on the gauge beside the faraway reservoir to see when heavy usage dropped the water level to the point that auxiliary pumps should be started.[55]

Fast-increasing demand for water, though, presented the biggest challenge. In 1885 Brackenridge had a mile-long raceway dug to a new pumphouse with a stronger pump that could supply the reservoir with three million gallons a day. To increase the flow even more, steam-driven pumps were added at both pumphouses. In 1887 an auxiliary reservoir half the size of the main one was built downgrade to the southwest, its site now covered by the botanical garden's main parking area.[56]

In the mid-1880s drought lowered the Edwards Aquifer's supply of water to the San Antonio River. Already water-starved regions in the western United States were increasing their use of artesian wells to supplement surface water, since the wells yielded a seemingly unlimited supply. In 1887–88 the first artesian wells in San Antonio were drilled into the Austin Chalk Aquifer near the West End subdivision and filled what is now called Woodlawn Lake. Brackenridge believed that having such a well next to his main reservoir could spill water directly into the reservoir, eliminating the need for the two pumphouses. In 1888 he dug one, its shaft still preserved beside the main reservoir's north wall. Notably, that well was the first to tap the massive Edwards Aquifer. But it was of no use, for artesian pressure was insufficient to force the water as far up as the reservoir, and it was too deep to pump successfully.[57]

The main water works reservoir appears at top (*right center*) in this aerial view from about 1920, below the smaller auxiliary reservoir that became the botanical garden's East Texas lake. In the lower image, outside the main reservoir's restored wall at far left is the top of the pioneering but unsuccessful artesian well once intended to supply the reservoir.

"I remember as well as if it were yesterday our disappointment over the first well," Hallet E. Ellsworth, then Water Works secretary, recalled three decades later. "It cost the company, which meant Mr. Brackenridge, $10,000 to prove that it was a duster. The well was a miserable failure, and the money was entirely lost."[58]

In 1891 Brackenridge tried drilling at a lower elevation near the southwest corner of Market Street and the San Antonio River. That well produced such a gusher that the Water Works Company drilled eight more wells nearby and established a pumping station at the site, still active today. Unexpected droughts made river water unreliable for the growing city's needs, so in 1892 artesian wells were drilled in Brackenridge Park and linked to the two pumphouses. At that point San Antonio's water supply shifted entirely to artesian water. Water storage at a new tank some sixty feet tall at the Market Street plant replaced regular use of the old stone reservoir, still kept full for backup should pumps fail to function. Every few months pumping purposely overflowed the reservoir's stagnant water to spill accumulated debris over the top, and once a year it was drained for cleaning.[59]

The water-driven pumphouse and reservoir system became fully obsolete in 1915 with construction of a major pumping station in southeastern Brackenridge Park by a successor company to George Brackenridge's San Antonio Water Works. But the new pumping station's underground engine house continued to keep the old reservoir full for backup for as long as another decade.[60]

Components of the old water system were creatively repurposed. The 1878 pumphouse spent its early retirement years as a bathhouse for adjacent Lambert Beach. Sculptor Gutzon Borglum used the 1885 pumphouse as a studio and designed prototypes for Mount Rushmore there. And the stone reservoir, mostly intact, eventually became an amphitheater for the San Antonio Botanical Garden.

Once water fit for drinking could be piped up hills and over rises, San Antonio's municipal development mushroomed. One no longer needed to live downgrade from the San Antonio River or San Pedro Creek to receive water diverted from the two streams into Spanish-era acequias. New residents pouring in by rail since the late 1870s more than doubled the city's population to fifty-three thousand by 1900, when San Antonio overtook Dallas to become the largest city in Texas.

Growth was further aided by the opening in 1890 of the city's first large electrical plant, able to power electric streetcars for quick transportation miles from downtown. Property values went up especially on high ground, where cool breezes offered summertime relief from the sultry city below. "Heights" and "hill" became real estate buzzwords. Prospect Hill was developed on the west side of town, Laurel Heights and—a semantic stretch—Monte Vista on the north, and Denver Heights on the east.

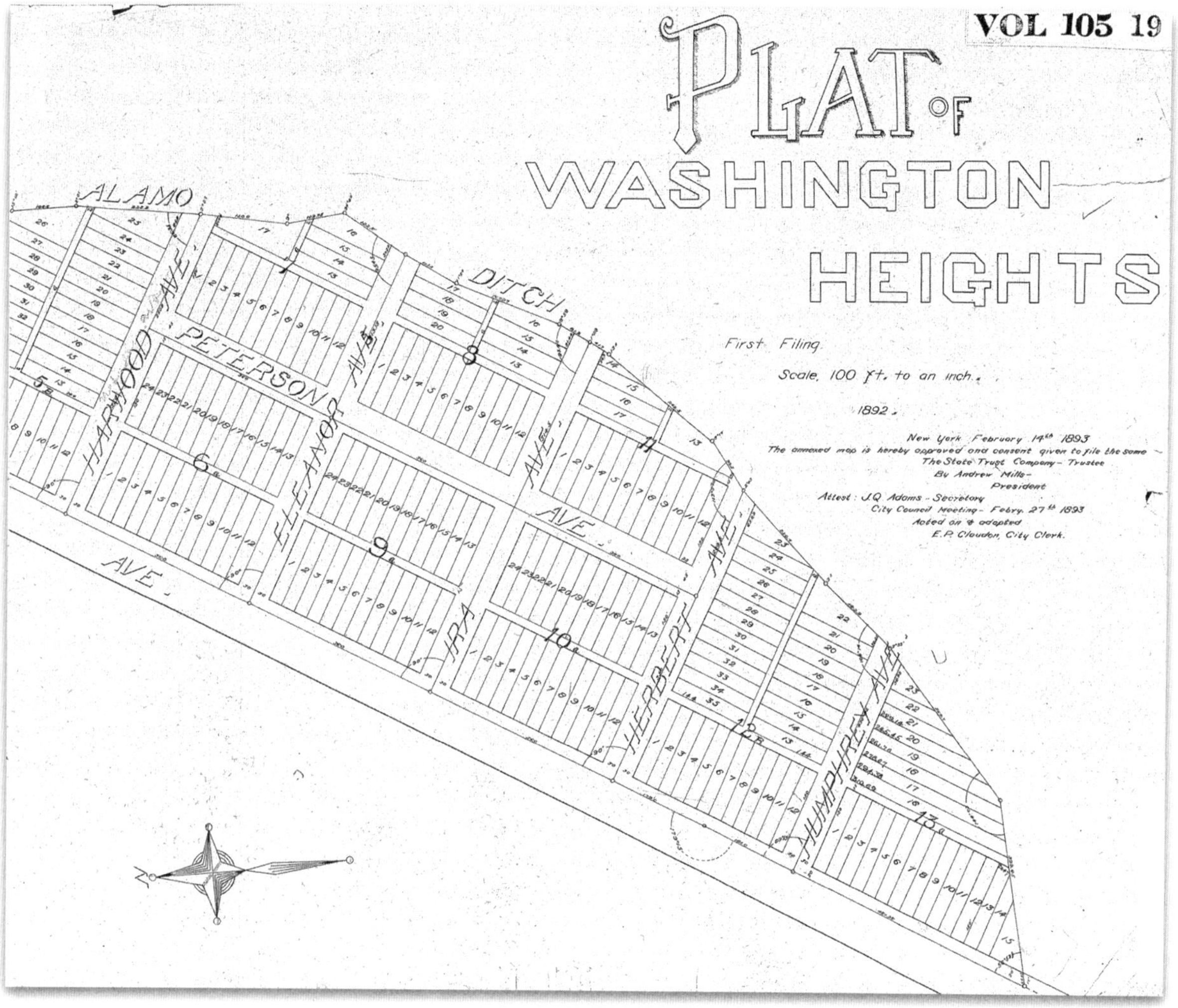

George Brackenridge sold most of the 1,200 acres around the reservoir to a Denver developer. The only portion platted before the developer's bankruptcy in 1893 was between River Avenue / Broadway and the Alamo Acequia.

The opportunity was catnip to Colorado's Chamberlain Investment Company, which the *New York Times* termed "the largest real estate company in the west." To help snare distant investors, the company president officed in London and the treasurer in New York City. A guiding principle was to pay low prices for large, difficult to reach tracts on the fringes of cities and build electric streetcar lines to connect the tracts with downtowns, then to reap large profits by selling lots for newly accessible residential development.[61]

In 1890 the Denver-based company bought three large tracts in San Antonio, the two largest of which were north of downtown. One was 1,500 acres of "beautifully diversified upland" three miles from the center of town, the former ranchland of Hiram H. McLane. His onetime home became the Argyle Hotel and Chamberlain's subsidiary Alamo Heights Land and Improvement Company began selling building lots around a stylish street plan. Since Alamo Heights was yet beyond the reach of San Antonio's water system, Chamberlain drilled wells to establish a private water company. The company helped finance extension of River Avenue / Broadway to Alamo Heights, and in August 1890 it built a streetcar line along that route that connected with existing lines.[62]

The Alamo Heights line conveniently passed Chamberlain's second purchase in San Antonio, 1,200 acres bought from George Brackenridge located roughly between River Avenue / Broadway on the west, Salado Creek on the east, Burr Road on the north, and Fort Sam Houston on the south. The purchased tract, which surrounded the hilltop reservoir, was named Washington Heights. Chamberlain's subsidiary Washington Heights Land Company's main activity in 1892–93 was platting dozens of lots along ten new short streets off River Avenue between present-day Pershing and Brackenridge Avenues. The streets extended the brief distance from River Avenue east to the western bank of the Alamo Acequia and had the advantage of ample water from the reservoir up the hill. The company continued to purchase small additional tracts from Brackenridge.[63]

In the mostly vacant Washington Heights land awaiting development, one tenant took advantage of the absence of homeowners who might object to noise. In 1892 the San Antonio Shooting Company purchased nearly twelve acres across North New Braunfels Avenue from the future botanical garden, between present-day Queen Anne Court and Elmhurst Avenue. This was the local German community's shooting club, established in 1857 as San Antonio Schuetzen Verein. In 1892 the club obtained a permit for a rifle range and a shooting stand, which it later expanded to four stands and a clubhouse. It held target practice and shooting matches in Washington Heights until new homes came closer; remaining members sold the property and disbanded in 1919.[64]

Washington Heights Land Company stock was being offered "at a great bargain" in mid-1892, but the entire Chamberlain empire collapsed during the Panic of 1893. Chamberlain's Alamo Heights Land and Improvement Company took six years to sort things out, though the Washington Heights Land Company resolved its indebtedness in less time. Its assets were acquired by the Washington Heights Improvement Company, chartered in May 1898 with George Brackenridge as its president. Land sales resumed.[65]

The lower portion of Mahncke Park has had few improvements since its creation in 1905.

The Curious Case of Mahncke Park

What is usually thought of as Mahncke Park begs the question of why the city made a park out of land too wide to be a median for the flanking streets but too narrow to become a significant park.

Few now realize, and no signage reveals, that Mahncke Park consists of not only the thirteen-acre, mesquite-studded hillside strip between Brackenridge Park on Broadway and North New Braunfels Avenue; it also continues across North New Braunfels to comprise most of the home of the magnificent San Antonio Botanical Garden, now covering thirty-nine acres.

What is today commonly considered Mahncke Park is hardly one-fourth of the awkwardly shaped park's actual size.

How the oft-neglected park was created and survived long enough to be discovered as a distinctive site for a botanical garden is the story of a phantom boulevard, municipal indifference, and several attempts at dismembering the park—one of them successful—a tale until now virtually untold.

At the beginning of the twentieth century San Antonio was the largest city in Texas. Fast-growing competitors like Dallas and Houston showed off their prosperity by funding handsome parks and civic amenities designed by nationally known professionals. But cash-poor San Antonio was not about to hire expensive designers funded by taxes so many residents didn't want to pay. In 1904 the City of Dallas hired the eminent city planner and landscape architect George Kessler for the first of his redesigns of the city's major elements, including its park system and boulevards. In those years, if similar work was desired in San Antonio,

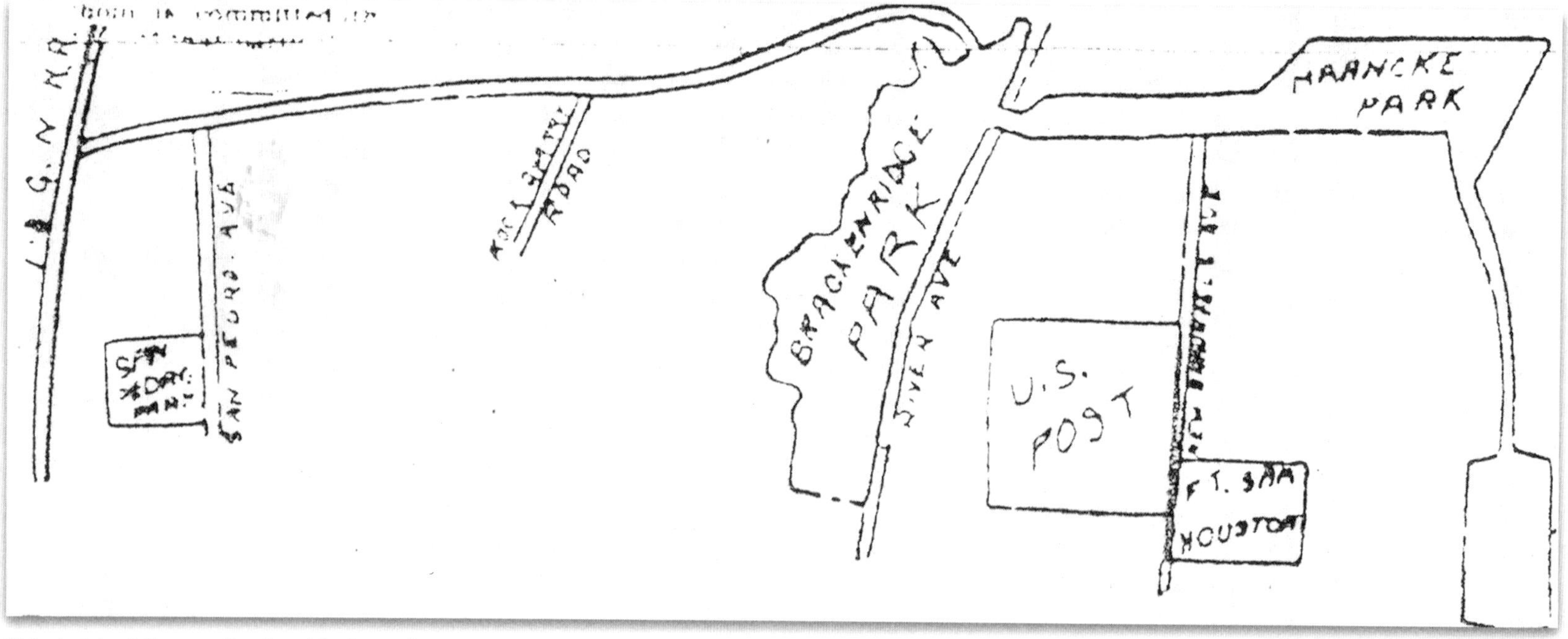

This sketch of George Brackenridge's northeastern section of a boulevard proposed to circle the city appeared in the *Express* in 1905.

untrained citizens would have to do it on their own. George Brackenridge was among them.

In 1899 Brackenridge and his San Antonio Water Works Company donated some two hundred riverside acres to the city. The gift was named Brackenridge Park, by far the largest park in the city. Its simple design was drawn, perhaps on a kitchen table, by Brackenridge, a banker and financier; the mayor, Marshall Hicks, a lawyer; and Ludwig Mahncke, who ran a beer garden and hotel before becoming the city's park commissioner.[66]

Now that they had a large park, San Antonians wished they had a scenic boulevard system like other big cities were getting. In 1905 Brackenridge stepped up again, joining others in making plans for a landscaped boulevard circling fifteen miles around the city, a nice jaunt for those driving the newly popular automobiles.

Brackenridge's contribution would be the northern and northeastern sections. From San Pedro Avenue the boulevard would head eastward along the general path of present-day Hildebrand Avenue and cut south through wooded Brackenridge Park to River Avenue / Broadway. From there it would head east up to the water works reservoir and turn south to meet another section of the loop near the Southern Pacific railyard.[67]

His part of the drive would be scenic, Brackenridge asserted, for it followed "the most beautiful heights around San Antonio," offering "at every turn of the road magnificent views" of the city. A difficult crossing at River Avenue / Broadway and Brackenridge Park would be avoided by "a handsome brick and stone bridge of rustic type," a "thing of great architectural beauty" complete with a fountain and vines. Right of way would not be a problem, Brackenridge said, as he owned all of the land for his segment east of the park and had favorable indications for "an arrangement" from owners of the five sections of the route west of the park. "The entire proposition can be arranged easily with perhaps a small bond issue," he believed.[68]

In addition, Brackenridge promised to donate two parks along his segment for the boulevard to pass through, offering stops for strolling or picnicking. In May 1905 he demonstrated his seriousness by giving the city the first of the two, between

North New Braunfels Avenue and Austin Road. That included the four acres forming the reservoir tract, which he donated personally and as president of the Water Works Company, and twenty-five surrounding acres, which he gave personally and as president of the Washington Heights Improvement Company. He asked that the park be named to honor his friend Ludwig Mahncke, the longtime park commissioner. City commissioners happily complied.[69]

Two weeks later Brackenridge further proved his commitment to the boulevard by giving an adjacent section, a brushy fifteen-acre strip the width of the proposed boulevard—three hundred feet—from North New Braunfels Avenue down the slope to River Avenue / Broadway, where the thoroughfare would cross the proposed bridge into Brackenridge Park. This section was to be named Campbell Boulevard after the incumbent reform mayor, John Campbell, first elected to public office in 1878 as the city's animal hide inspector. Until the boulevard was constructed, the strip would be considered an extension of Mahncke Park.[70]

The route of Campbell Boulevard / lower Mahncke Park was dictated by the immovable placement of the main reservoir. The crossing from Brackenridge Park was located so that, in following a straight line up the hillside, the boulevard's northern edge came no closer to the reservoir than the southern edge of the berm surrounding it. As the thoroughfare crossed below the reservoir and turned southeast, its path sliced off approximately a third of Brackenridge's original land donation, leaving the northern twenty acres or so with the reservoir and beyond to become the final Mahncke Park.

A complication for the Water Works Company, which remained in operation, was that the boulevard would sever the connection between the main reservoir and the auxiliary stone reservoir, southwest down the slope near the corner of North New Braunfels Avenue and Pinckney Street and outside the land donation's southern boundary. Brackenridge's solution was to replace the smaller reservoir with a reservoir lake north of the main reservoir. Dug nineteen feet into the caliche in 1905 and lined with clay, it connected to the main reservoir by an overflow pipe. The lake would double as a water feature for the new park.[71]

Mahncke Park was named for Ludwig Mahncke, George Brackenridge's friend and longtime park commissioner.

The site of the earthen reservoir lake was repurposed decades later as the San Antonio Botanical Garden's East Texas lake.

In giving the two tracts of land, Brackenridge included the restriction, famously made in his earlier donation of Brackenridge Park, that the city "shall never permit any beer or intoxicating liquor of any kind to be sold, given away or drunk within any part of said premises." Failure to promptly address

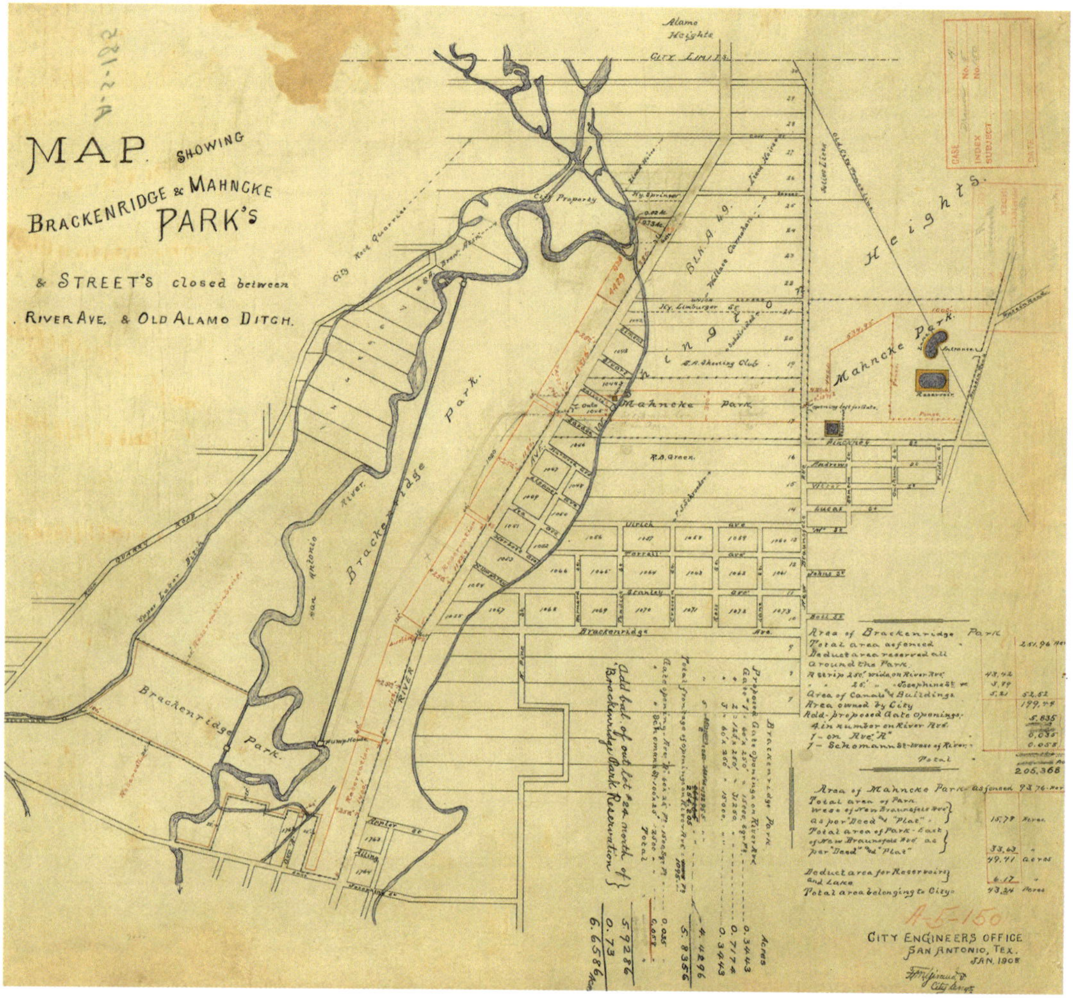

Mahncke Park's section east of New Braunfels Avenue (*center right*), mapped in 1908, is now occupied by the San Antonio Botanical Garden, which encompasses the three reservoirs.

any violation would require the city to "at once" surrender ownership of the park to the state for the benefit of the University of Texas, Brackenridge's favorite charity, which he long served as a regent. As he had with Brackenridge Park, Brackenridge reserved continued ownership of all improvements and the right to add additional ones, "whether for supplying water to the city and its inhabitants or for irrigating purposes."[72]

The upper park's irregular northern and western boundaries left Brackenridge and his Washington Heights Improvement Company with adjoining land to sell for development. The northwestern corner outside the border between Parland Place and Pershing Avenue became a residential area named Northview Addition. The southern boundary extended from North New Braunfels Avenue to Austin Road. It later formed the center line for the extension of Funston Place.

But despite Brackenridge's efforts and donations of land, neither his boulevard proposal nor the plans of others who followed came to fruition. In 1913 Brackenridge sold three hundred acres on the proposed route east of Mahncke Park to the federal government. It became a key tract of Camp Travis, an annex to Fort Sam Houston, where thirty-one thousand officers and men organized as the Ninetieth Division for World

A 1920s storm caused collapse of the army's Austin Road repair shop across from the future botanical garden in Fort Sam Houston's sprawling Camp Travis.

War I. The name of Mayor John Campbell, who did not run for reelection in 1905, disappeared from the boulevard site. Mahncke Park's lower extension, undeveloped, was yet referred to for years to come as Mahncke Boulevard.[73]

With the much larger Brackenridge Park next door still having as many opportunities for development as the parks department could deal with, the city could not figure out what to do with Mahncke Park. To keep from having to maintain it for public use, the city erected wire fences around its borders; only the caretaker could enter the padlocked "semi-ornamental" gate. A reporter sent to investigate in 1911 found that "there never was such a nondescript place as Mahncke Park," its "matted undergrowth" infested with cactus and turned into "a dumping ground" by intruders who littered the place with "sheet iron and debris."[74]

There were those who thought something should be done. In mid-1913 the civic committee of the city's Federation of Women's Clubs proposed that "Mahncke Park be laid out and planted this winter," since, out of gratitude to its donor, "it should be properly beautified and thrown open to the public." Mayor Clinton Brown favored turning the park into a municipal nine-hole golf course if it wouldn't cost the city anything. That idea became moot two years later when the city built an eighteen-hole course filling the lower half of Brackenridge Park.[75]

In 1915, his first year as parks commissioner, Ray Lambert requested $5,000 to build driveways and beautify Mahncke Park. But nothing seems to have been done, perhaps due to Lambert's distractions building the golf course, Japanese Tea Garden, and zoo. Twelve years later Lambert and Mayor John Tobin rejected a petition from nearby residents to beautify Mahncke Park, claiming that "there is no money in the treasury for further park work" but promising that "the park will be kept free from undergrowth by city prisoners on the chain gang." A victim of its irregular shape and overshadowed by its proximity to the popular Brackenridge Park, Mahncke Park was left, the *San Antonio Express* concluded, as "a sort of stepchild in the city's park system."[76]

Though the city had little use for Mahncke Park, officials doubtless feared the political repercussions of any attempt to dispose of dedicated parkland for incompatible purposes, other than those of the sacrosanct U.S. military, which underpinned the city's economy. So officials apparently took the path of shrinking the problem by taking every opportunity to dismember the park for the least controversial reasons.

By 1934 the main stone reservoir and nearby reservoir lake (*center right*) were unused and empty, as was the original backup reservoir, outlined by trees (*below far left center*). Fort Sam Houston housing units (*lower right*) replaced that part of Camp Travis.

In 1915 the city saw no harm in slicing off sixty feet of the lower park's width—totaling about three acres—as the municipal contribution to rights of way for new streets alongside the park between Broadway and North New Braunfels Avenue. Houses facing an improved park would have a more impressive view than those in the surrounding area, thus encouraging construction of finer homes on larger lots. That justified naming the roadways "place" rather than the less prestigious "street" or "avenue" like those developing nearby. Parland Place was built along the park's northern edge, Funston Place along the southern.[77]

Nine years later the city tried to lop off the entire upper part of the park, east of North New Braunfels Avenue and adjacent to Fort Sam Houston, by offering it to the National Guard for a cavalry headquarters. But with the inclusion of strings like the city's right "to take possession of the land whenever it desires it for park purposes," the National Guard did not accept.[78]

Mahncke Park seemed poised for improvement in 1934, when the Civil Works Administration sent three hundred workers to turn the former main reservoir into a sunken garden and tier the lower slope to Broadway for cascading water. But months later the agency shut down and its successor, the Works Progress Administration, did not pursue the project. Nor was the Business and Professional Women's Club able to convert the lower section into a botanical garden.[79]

Back at square one, in 1940 the city tried again to donate the upper part of the park by offering it as a headquarters site for the U.S. Army's Eighth Corps, whose commander, Maj. Gen. Walter Krueger, felt that Fort Sam Houston lacked sufficient space for its headquarters to remain in San Antonio. The army surveyed the tract, but Krueger ultimately declined the offer and moved his headquarters to Camp Bowie at Brownwood.[80]

Two years later the city sliced a strip from the upper end of Mahncke Park by striking a deal with investors Luther Hodges and William Ochse Jr. As it had for the new streets beside the lower park, the city provided half of the right of way to extend Funston Place from North New Braunfels Avenue east to Austin Road, along the park's southern border. The investors donated the other half. That enabled construction of Hilltop Terraces, a row of low-cost duplexes for families of wartime workers at Fort Sam Houston. It was an incursion the San Antonio Botanical Garden would go to great lengths to reverse seven decades later.[81]

The city was also agreeable to another proposal that would have eliminated a third of lower Mahncke Park and as much as a third of the upper park as well.

By 1945 Charline Street, later renamed Milton Street, had been cut across the park between Funston and Parland Place some four hundred yards east of Broadway, easing the route to Lamar Elementary School on Parland for students who lived south of the park. The segment between Charline / Milton Street and Broadway, a third of lower Mahncke Park, happened to suit the City Water Board, which was looking in 1957 for a site for a multistory headquarters building and parking for 150 vehicles. Additionally, a storage tank for eighty million gallons of water—sixteen times the capacity of the old reservoir—would be built in the upper park on the site of the former reservoir lake. The utility claimed that it had the authority to unilaterally take the sites since Brackenridge had reserved the right of his water company and its successors to use park property for future needs.[82]

"We have never looked on Mahncke Park as a true park," explained water board manager Robert A. Thompson Jr., "since Brackenridge Park is directly across the street. The city has done nothing with the park, and nothing is planned for it. We don't feel our exercising of our right to use it would interfere with the general public welfare."[83]

Neighbors erupted in opposition. "Keep Off!" warned an editorial in the *Light*. School officials joined in concern

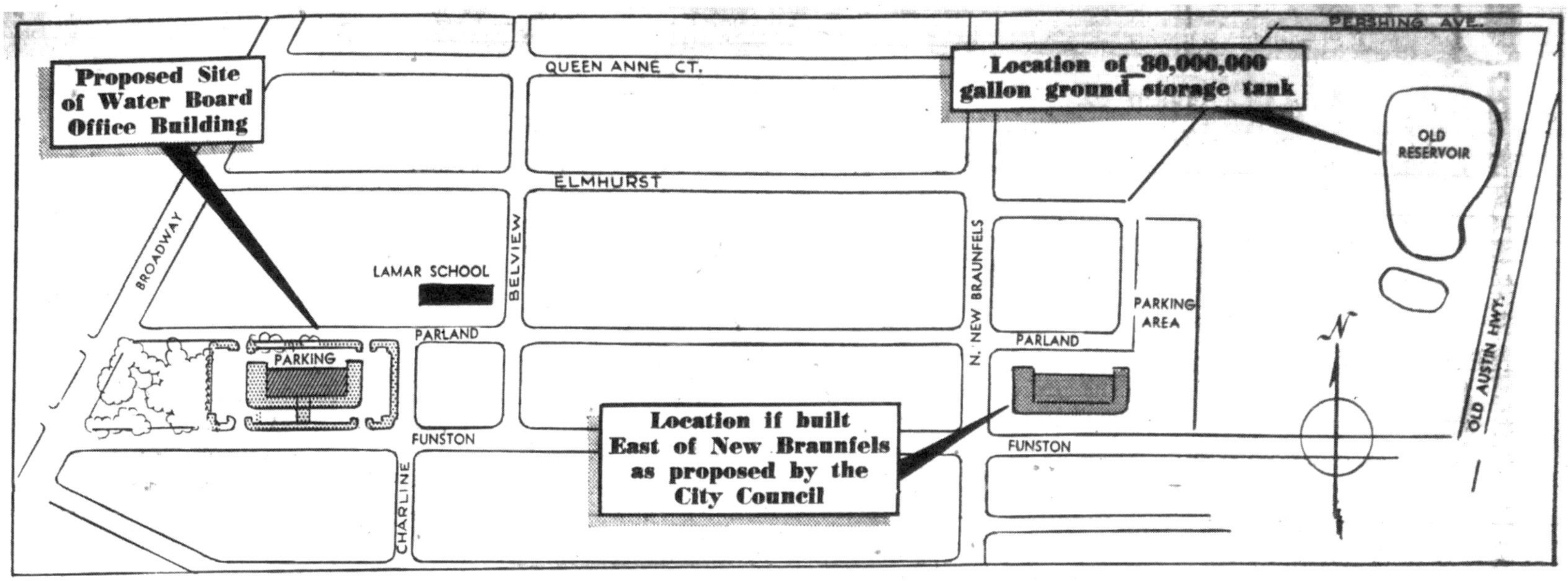

Had 1957 plans by the City Water Board succeeded, upper Mahncke Park would have shrunk, making it unviable for the botanical garden site.

for student safety at the nearby school. The San Antonio Conservation Society opposed commercial construction in any park. The water board's counterproposal that the building instead be in the upper section of Mahncke Park, on the North New Braunfels Avenue spot the San Antonio Garden Center was eyeing for its building, did not assuage opponents. The office building, parking lot, and water storage tank would have effectively ended the upper section's potential for meaningful park use. Two years later the proposal was withdrawn.[84]

The way was clear for the San Antonio Garden Center's second try for its headquarters building and for a botanical garden in upper Mahncke Park.

Shaping the Botanical Garden

A September 1978 vista from the botanical garden's overlook shows emerging pathways, gardens, and meadows, with the new entry building at center opening onto a fountain plaza. World War II–era housing lines the far side of Funston Place (*left*).

Preparing the Site

By the time Mayor John Gatti snipped a flower-trimmed ribbon and celebrants entered the San Antonio Garden Center's newly dedicated building in October 1966, the center's botanical garden committee had been at work for at least five years. The assumed location for the garden was Mahncke Park's narrow thirteen-acre lower section, where earlier suggestions had culminated with its designation by the city council for a botanical garden in 1934.

The site seemed so assured that Anna Mahncke Deutz, daughter of park namesake Ludwig Mahncke, donated $7,500—today's equivalent of $75,000—for a circular concrete fountain with high dancing waters at the foot of Mahncke Park along Broadway. The fountain, dedicated in June 1964, was reported as a focal point of the planned botanical garden. Four years later it was joined nearby by a monument to Ludwig Mahncke that had been done by prominent sculptor Pompeo Coppini in 1908. The monument was originally intended for that spot until Mahncke Park—then fenced, locked, and overgrown—was deemed an unsuitable location. Its interim location had been near the onetime Jockey Club clubhouse on what became the Brackenridge Park Golf Course.[85]

Little-used lower Mahncke Park seemed to be such an obvious site for improvement as a botanical garden that it did not come to the average viewer's mind that the park's less visible and derelict upper thirty-two acres might be better. A survey in 1976 reported that for years that space had been "an unofficial dumping ground" and that "the dense undergrowth and countless mounds of trash and building refuse have masked any undisturbed surfaces which may have existed after the reservoir was abandoned. . . . Piles of broken building material form a mantle over much of the area. Several small gravel roads weave in and out of the overgrown area around the reservoir and provide access to those individuals responsible for dumping."[86]

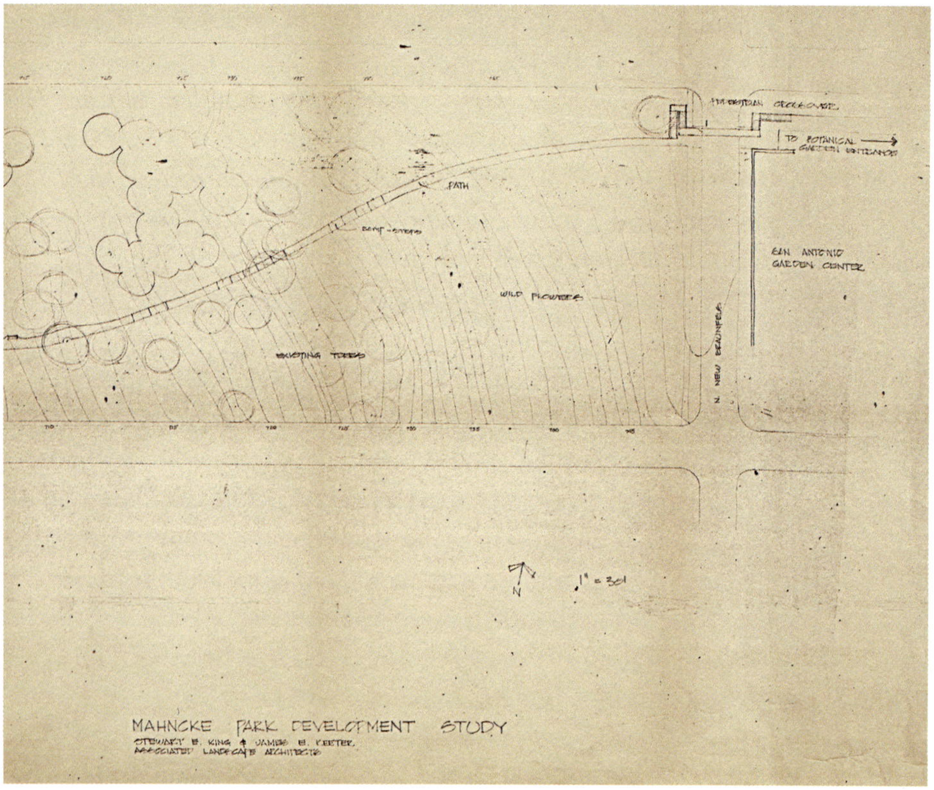

In 1967 the garden center retained landscape architects Stewart King and his associate James E. Keeter to prepare plans for a botanical garden and arboretum in Mahncke Park. A walkway would go over North New Braunfels Avenue to the arboretum in the lower park.

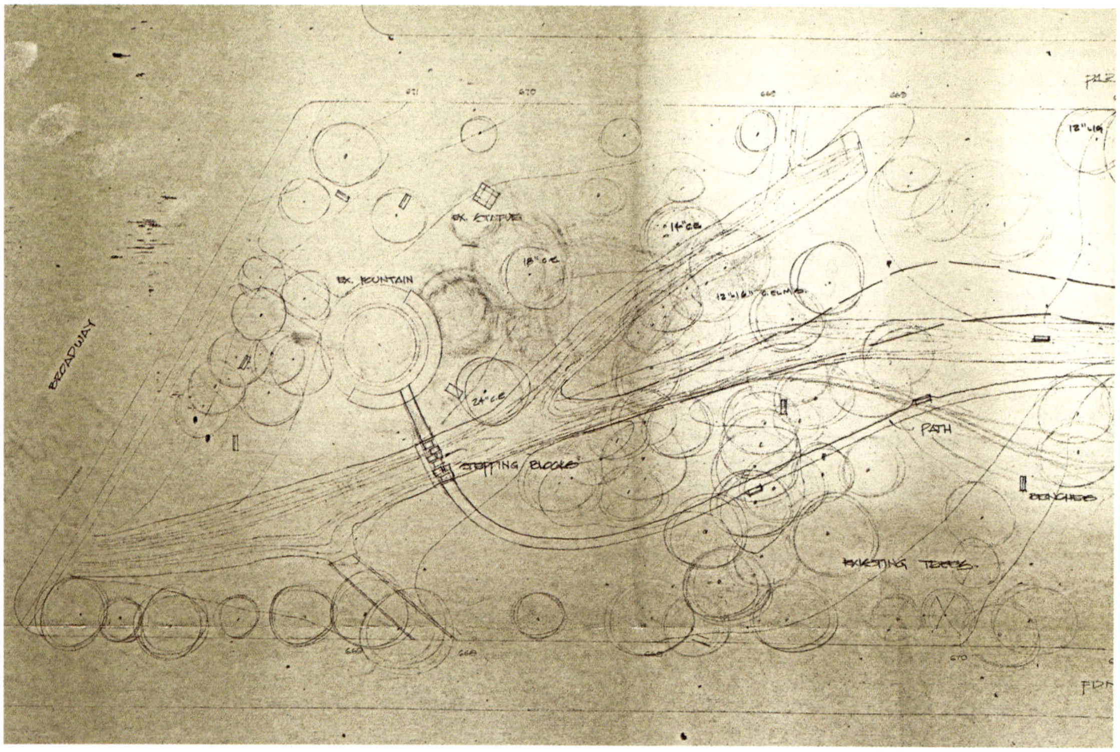

But at some point in the mid-1960s, as planners studied the subject more carefully, they shifted the botanical garden site to that area. The squarish upper park portion, while perhaps in need of a thorough cleanup, would be more efficient to use than the narrow portion of the park below, and had more varied natural contours.

"This site was a very good choice in our region for a botanical garden," said Andrew Labay, chief mission officer of the San Antonio Botanical Garden. "The depth of the Blackland clay soil goes down as far as five to six feet in places before reaching the caliche base. It provides good fertility, although in some locations it can retain too much water, limiting the growth of such sensitive plants as succulents." But, he added, "being on a high point means that during freezes the coldest air drains down the slopes, providing slightly elevated temperatures that can be beneficial. And the varied terrain allows creation of beautiful landscapes not possible on a flat site."[87]

A likely candidate for having made the site breakthrough is Stewart King, a landscape architect retained by the garden center in 1967. With the center settled in its new building, he was asked to draw up a site plan for the botanical garden. A onetime landscape architect with the U.S. Army Corps of Engineers and the National Park Service, King was San Antonio's parks and recreation director for twelve years, until 1951, when he began private practice in office space shared with noted San Antonio architect O'Neil Ford. King's projects ranged from HemisFair Plaza to Austin's Town Lake development and the garrison area at White Sands Missile Range. Earlier he had presented the design problem of Mahncke Park as a botanical garden to a senior landscape design class he taught at Louisiana State University.[88]

At the same time the parks department, which would be doing the work, was looking at botanical gardens throughout the nation. It focused on the fifty-two-acre Brooklyn Botanic Garden, designed by Olmsted Brothers in 1910, as having features that would best fit San Antonio. A delegation from the city spent several days there. One concept successfully applied in San Antonio was that of a children's vegetable garden similar to the one established at the Brooklyn garden in 1914.[89]

In December 1967 King and his protégé, James E. Keeter, completed a "very basic, preliminary" plan that contained many features of the present garden, though not all in the same places. The estimated cost of completion was $265,000, approximately $1.9 million today. That passed muster with the Parks and Recreation Subcommittee for Capital Improvements, which endorsed including that amount in the city's $65.5 million bond issue package, approved by voters in September 1970.[90]

Some reports indicate that lower Mahncke Park was also included in the project. A second schematic drawing by King and Keeter portrayed that area as an arboretum with wildflowers, additional trees, picnic tables, and a bridge, all linked by a sinuous sidewalk ending at the fountain at the foot of the park, where pedestrians could enter from Broadway. At the upper end King connected the two parts of Mahncke Park with a pedestrian bridge over North New Braunfels Avenue. Work on the lower section, however, did not occur.[91]

Despite momentum from the successful bond vote, the botanical project remained stalled for four years, apparently due to the need for additional funding. The only progress that can be detected came in 1972, when the parks department retained two former associates of King, who had died a month before the bond vote at age sixty-three. The associates retained were Keeter and George G. Cook. The two reissued the 1969 master plan map produced by King and Keeter, changing its attribution to Keeter and Cook, but apparently did little else. Management of the Parks and Recreation Department changed as longtime director Robert Fraser retired in 1973 and was followed by Ronald Darner, age thirty.[92]

The inaction left an opportunity for others to muscle in.

The Beautify San Antonio Association, a branch of the Greater San Antonio Chamber of Commerce, announced in 1974 that it was making its annual project "Beautify San Antonio Botanical Gardens." A mailing under the signatures of project cochairs A. C. Crouch and Chalmer Gamblin, a former president of the Garden Center, sought $100,000 to erect within the proposed botanical garden a Patio of States, for which "every governor is sending to San Antonio a large flat stone (native of their state)" to be carved into the shape of their state. The carved stones would be pieced together to form a map of the United States 240 feet wide. "There is no other such patio in the world," the senders asserted. Behind the patio, granite walkways would surround a large fountain with, beyond, "some 50 patios of every kind of tree and plants." The gardens would be "dedicated to beautification" and named, the writers hoped, "in honor of the Beautify San Antonio Association."[93]

The mailing announced that opening ceremonies would occur on October 1, 1974, and that Lady Bird Johnson and Texas governor Dolph Briscoe would be asked to preside.[94]

Whatever diverted that scheme, the patio effort moved to the Hilton Palacio del Rio Hotel and then across the street to the convention center, where a version of the Patio of States was built in 1976 as a bicentennial project. The San Antonio Bicentennial Celebration Committee awarded Beautify San Antonio Association founder O. P. Schnabel a certificate honoring him for "his Patio of States project."[95]

Whether or not it was the Beautify San Antonio Association's gambit that spurred Gilbert Denman Jr., chair of the Ewing Halsell Foundation, to action, his imagination had been captured by the concept of a botanical garden. Though Denman does not seem to have been involved in the garden initiatives earlier, he thought it was time to be "getting the project moving." Armed with the sort of foundation financial portfolio prior garden visionaries could only have dreamed of, Denman contacted parks department director Ron Darner in 1974 to discuss the situation.[96]

Gilbert Morgan Denman Jr., then fifty-five, was a third-generation member of the law firm that had represented George Brackenridge, who had donated Mahncke Park to the city. Denman was an aide to Fleet Adm. Chester Nimitz during World War II, served as chair of the board of Trinity University, and assembled and donated the collection that launched the San Antonio Museum of Art's galleries of ancient Mediterranean art. The galleries were housed, not coincidentally, in the museum's Ewing Halsell Wing.

In 1974 Gilbert M. Denman Jr., chair of the Ewing Halsell Foundation, got the botanical garden project moving.

The Ewing Halsell Foundation funded this model to help visualize the botanical garden project. The proposed four-room hexagonal conservatory (*front center*) was scuttled when the present facility, to be at lower right, was conceived.

Ewing and Lucile Halsell, Oklahoma natives with ranching and oil interests who had moved to San Antonio, had established the Ewing Halsell Foundation in 1957 to make "impactful" grants in San Antonio and South Texas. After Ewing Halsell's death in 1965 the foundation was chaired by their friend Denman. The thoughtful and self-effacing Denman was described in the *San Antonio Express-News* as "the ultimate insider" in San Antonio's world of arts and culture, one who, "as the English say, was 'a man who could put his hands on all the ropes.'" It is no exaggeration to say that Denman was the individual most responsible for the San Antonio Botanical Garden's rise to excellence.[97]

To the parks director's delight, after their meeting in 1974 Denman pledged $100,000 in Ewing Halsell Foundation funds to elevate garden plans for the eleven northeastern acres of Mahncke Park, a third of the total area. Rather than the planned but unremarkable designations for native plantings, an "aquatic area," and a "meditation garden," Denman suggested a carefully configured area replicating natural settings of three distinctive regions of Texas—East Texas, South Texas, and the Hill Country.

As Denman intended, the gift shook the project out of limbo. Keeter and Cook updated the master site map, and the Ewing Halsell Foundation funded a scale model so others

Groundbreaking occurred on July 21, 1976, at the site of the Garden for the Blind. From left are Grady Price and Angeleta Sanchez of the Governor's Commission for the Blind, Mayor Pro Tem Al Rohde, mule driver Bartolo Garcia, and the Von Ormy nurseryman who provided the mule.

could visualize the plan. The fledgling University of Texas at San Antonio Center for Archaeological Research prepared a site assessment that found no evidence of prehistoric occupation, clearing the way for construction.[98]

On July 21, 1976, a mule and plow brought from a nursery in Von Ormy, ten miles south of San Antonio, broke ground for the botanical garden on the site chosen for a Garden for the Blind, where plantings were planned with large features or strong aromas that could be detected by those with vision issues. Assisting the mule driver were Mayor ProTem Al Rohde and two representatives of the Texas Commission for the Blind. The Most Rev. Patrick Flores, auxiliary bishop of the Catholic Archdiocese of San Antonio, gave the invocation, and the Rev. Earl Bissex, pastor of Alamo Heights Christian Church, delivered the benediction. A reception followed at the garden center.[99]

The parks department did its best to incorporate as many elements of Keeter and Cook's plan as finances allowed to be ready for opening day, three and a half years away. The site was scraped clean of the decades of accumulated rubble and refuse, which were then heaped and sodded over to create an overlook at the garden's highest point. A frame gazebo at the peak offered a view of the San Antonio skyline. From there a reproduced

Workers complete a wooden pavilion in 1977. It was later replaced by a steel tempietto atop the overlook, which had been created with bulldozed rubble previously dumped on the garden site.

The Garden for the Blind, funded by the San Antonio Garden Center and later renamed the Sensory Garden, was ready for the grand opening.

rock-lined acequia flowed downward to the main grounds, reminding visitors of San Antonio's earliest water system.

Remains of the 1878 reservoir nearby were partly filled and repaired as an amphitheater for classes and entertainment, with seating on stone steps inside one end. To its east, along Old Austin Road, a garden space was installed for seasonal use by children. At the southeast, in the area of the still unforeseen conservatory, went demonstration gardens and an aquatic area with koi swimming among tropical plantings.

The new garden's major structure was a modest hexagonal entrance building that allowed additions from the sides, with an administration/educational wing already sketched in to be added later. Its "antique features" included salvaged cypress doors with leaded and beveled glass. Walls had panels of similar beveled glass. The building was entered on its west side from the parking area off Funston Place directly behind the garden center headquarters, the parking area's waffle-like pavers interspersed with buffalo grass.[100]

The building's east entry opened onto a plaza featuring a low linear fountain of Mexican volcanic stone with water arcing from opposite sides into a central narrow rectangular pool, in the style of the Generalife Gardens fountain adjacent to the Alhambra in Granada, Spain. South of the entry building was the Garden for the Blind, underwritten by the garden center's contribution of the $55,000—some $200,000 today—which it had saved for such a facility.[101]

Garden center members had been inspired to include the Garden for the Blind by their success with the Lamplight Garden Club, formed in 1950 with nineteen vision-impaired gardeners and sponsored by the Woodlawn Hills Garden Club. The walled garden, designed with the aid of the Texas Commission for the Blind, included a handrail that led past a touchable ceramic relief model of features along the path. Plaques in braille and large print described plants with strong aromas and rich textures that could be felt and smelled at stops along the way. Topiaries provided large, dramatic shapes.[102]

Directly south of Fountain Plaza was the site for the originally planned conservatory, yet unfunded. Like the entrance building, it was to be hexagonal, with antique leaded and beveled glass. Its four exhibit rooms were to be covered by a standing-seam metal roof.[103]

On the northern side of Fountain Plaza, an arbor for wisteria led a few steps down to a series of gardens for flowering plants and herbs and a garden with plants mentioned in the Bible—figs, oleander, date palms, myrtle, violets. Beyond, in the garden's northwest corner, went a service area.

The most ambitious initial project took up the northeastern sector of the garden, replicating the natural environments of East Texas, South Texas, and the Hill Country. The sector's focal point would be a one-acre lake on the site of the water works auxiliary reservoir dug in 1905. The city used a 1977 windfall of $1 million in federal Economic Development Administration construction funding for H. B. Zachry Construction Company crews to scrape out debris, reshape the banks, line them with five thousand cubic yards of clay donated by USAA, and fill the lake with water. A fountain was added in the center for aeration.[104]

Further development of the Texas Native Area was covered by the $100,000 in Ewing Halsell Foundation funding engineered by Gilbert Denman Jr., who kept a close eye on how the Halsell money was spent. Parks director Darner sent detailed contractor invoices to Denman for approval, and parks department staff picked up the checks and processed them through the city's finance department. Denman kept current on the viability of plant selection through contacts like Danish-born Anders Saustrup, an energetic and wide-ranging scholar who at the time was field director of the Rare Plant Study Center at the University of Texas at Austin and was in touch with botanists throughout Texas. To be certain that the right plants were chosen, Denman and fellow Ewing Halsell Foundation trustee Helen Campbell, Halsell's former ranch secretary, paid Saustrup several visits.[105]

The Texas Native Area, focal point of the botanical garden's first major attraction, was once the city's auxiliary reservoir, its shore newly planted with saplings. A storage building was near a cabin with a deep porch, both part of an 1850s log farmstead disassembled in East Texas and rebuilt at the garden.

Denman envisioned the Texas Native Area not only as an open-air classroom featuring the flora and fauna of the three regions but also as a place "to illustrate the dependence of pioneer settlers on indigenous botanical material" in order to build their first homes in the wilderness. He saw to it that the Ewing Halsell Foundation's second major grant to the botanical garden—$71,900, some $350,000 today—covered reconstruction of an early East Texas log farmstead and a small, primitive native South Texas palisado dwelling.[106]

Overlooking the north bank of the East Texas lake went a grouping of four hand-hewn buildings that had been built in the 1850s near the East Texas community of Park, between La Grange and Fayetteville. Plentiful rainfall there, at the far edge of the nation's southeastern pine-hardwood forest, led to an abundance of trees that produced logs larger than elsewhere in the state.

The farmstead included a high-ceilinged cabin of post oak logs with a fireplace, a barn also of post oak logs, a storage building of cedar logs, a log smokehouse, and a stone well. Contractor Rudy Krisch III, who specialized in historic structures, indexed the structures' elements at their original site, dismantled them, and delivered the components to the garden in November 1976.[107]

Over the next two years Krisch's company repaired the cabin walls, reconstructed them using authentic tools and materials, treated logs with preservatives, and chinked the walls with clay, horsehair, and bark. The cabin's exterior lacked its original clapboards—left off to display the logs—and an interior loft was not put back due to fear of liability from potential attempts of visitors to climb up. New rafters and porch columns of red cedar cut onsite were joined with square nails and wooden pegs. New floors had sawed pine, and native cedar shake shingles made up the roofs. The reconstructed wraparound porch, deeply shaded to protect the original occupants from the sun, would prove ideal for future programs and demonstrations of pioneer crafts. A historical kitchen garden yielded vegetables, herbs, and fruit.[108]

The botanical garden's layer of clay topsoil over caliche posed a particular problem for East Texas plants needing a base of sandy loam and sandy clay. The solution came from Harris Sand Pits in Von Ormy, which at the beginning of 1978 supplied five thousand cubic yards of sandy soil to mimic the soil of East Texas.[109]

Once the soil was in place, parks department workers, using a two-ton truck, pickup, and rented backhoe, spent a week in deep East Texas north of Houston gathering five-foot trees donated by Sam Houston National Forest. They brought back forty-one loblolly pines, two shortleaf pines, six southern red oaks, six black oaks, two white oaks, three black tupelos, three Carolina buckthorns, three sassafras, two flatwood plums, one flowering dogwood, and one littlehip hawthorn. A dozen additional varieties were brought in a year later. Conroe's Lowery Nursery, an early specialist in native Texas plants, supplied shipments of East Texas shrubs and plants.[110]

To create an authentic pine forest floor, the parks department took dump trucks to Bastrop State Park and collected pine needle litter to cover the "East Texas" soil.[111]

"The biggest surprise to me was the reaction to the idea of constructing an East Texas forest outside its original range," Paul Cox recalled. He was fresh from graduate work in botany at Stephen F. Austin State University when San Antonio Parks and Recreation hired him as acting superintendent for horticultural services in 1977. He was transferred to the botanical garden to supervise horticultural development and research in 1980. "Many respected professionals leveled stinging criticism that the project would fail once the East Texas trees' roots grew deep enough to penetrate the sand, [then would] reach the clay and die." Even though transplanting the pines was difficult because of their extensive root system, "we had a high survival rate," Cox said.[112]

Over time, however, deepening root systems of some familiar East Texas trees such as pines and flowering dogwoods did struggle, according to the garden's Andrew Labay, "and now those trees are not as well represented in that area."[113]

The relatively flat and open section between the East Texas lake area and Old Austin Road was ideal for the South Texas native area. From the Fred Bruni Ranch in Zapata County, which bordered the Rio Grande, workers collected more than a dozen varieties of cactus, yucca, desert yaupon, cenizo, and blackbrush. More came from a ranch near Hondo. To compensate for the garden's incompatible soil and avoid the expense of having to cover it with a blanket of new soil as had been done in the East Texas section, enough sandy loam was brought in to make mounds for South Texas plantings. Although many plants were far north of their natural range and died back during hard freezes, they rebounded from their roots.[114]

The Ewing Halsell Foundation, which financed the move of the log farmstead from East Texas, also subsidized

A yucca blooms near a nineteenth-century stuccoed palisado cabin, representing South Texas in the Texas Native Area. A cutaway inside reveals the vertical cedar posts supporting the structure.

salvaging materials from an 1870s palisado home on Culebra Road west of Loop 410, more than ten miles from downtown San Antonio, and moving them to the garden's South Texas area.

The palisado house was in one sense a vertical log cabin. Its antique cedar posts were reset in the ground vertically and tied together horizontally with vines and sticks. The gaps between the posts were chinked with rocks and plastered with stucco on both sides, though workers left part of the interior wall unplastered to reveal the technique. A split cedar shake roof went on top.[115]

To the north, garden workers built a one-room adobe house—relatively cool in the summer—with blocks made of clay, sand, manure, and dried grass or straw that were air-dried, placed, and plastered. On the sod roof went the types of South Texas cacti and other native plants typically found growing from seeds carried by birds. A second room was added with walls of thin vertical sotol stalks supported by wood lath and twigs and a roof thatched with leaves of native palms.[116]

The two-room house, however, was ultimately removed. A year after the garden opening, contractors were having to make more "field alterations," and the adobe section was gone when Scott Litchke began working at the garden in 1991. The sotol room was left, though it was difficult to maintain. "We drove out to the country to find large sotol stalks to replace ones that had broken," Litchke said.

> We'd scramble up banks beside some road to get them, and no one questioned us because we had a Parks and Recreation Department truck. Then we'd take them back and prop up the [sotol room]. We'd also replace the palmetto palm fronds that covered the roof. But one day in about 1993 we looked and most of it had fallen down. I guess no one wanted to try rebuilding it, for soon it was just gone.[117]

The palisado house remained, though the original mud stucco exterior covering—which often gave visitors the mistaken impression that it was adobe—was replaced with an authentic-looking fiberglass covering that was far easier to maintain.[118]

Rougher terrain west of the botanical garden's East Texas lake area was suitable for the Hill Country area. Since the garden was in the first foothills of the Hill Country, many appropriate plants could be found close by. They were gathered at Brackenridge Park; the Alamo Cement Company location, part of which is now the Alamo Quarry Market shopping center; and Hill Country ranches. These plants ranged from agarita, bluebell, and Texas persimmon to prickly ash, live oak, and Uvalde maple. Most Hill Country plants, however, were accustomed to rocky soil that drained quickly. Planting them directly in the garden's dense caliche was a risk, and not all early plantings survived the waterlogged soil after heavy rains.[119]

To reflect one type of traditional architecture in the Hill Country, the Ewing Halsell Foundation designated funds in 1979 to purchase a compact three-room house

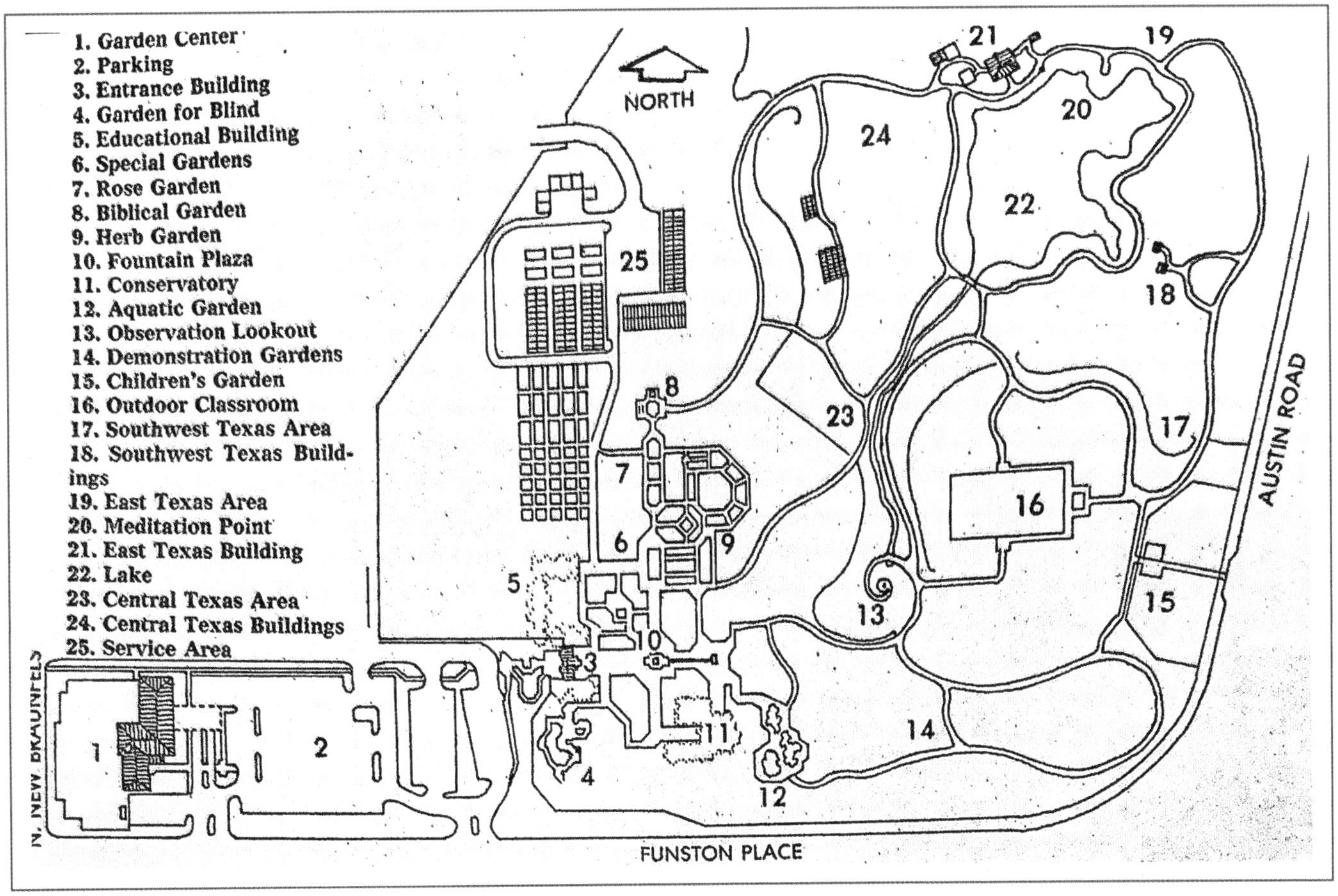

The botanical garden at its opening in May 1980.

in Fredericksburg. Scouted by James Keeter, the structure reflected the evolution of native building materials. It was disassembled and its pieces taken to await reconstruction on a gently rolling meadow at the northern edge of the Hill Country area. Tailor Friedrich Wilhelm Schumacher built the original one-room house in 1849 using German half-timber or *Fachwerk* construction, with filler of red clay, grass, and woven willow branches. A second room of post oak beams, rock infill, and mortar was added later, followed by a third room of quarried limestone with timbers that were no longer hand-hewn but sawed.[120]

South of the Schumacher house, at the edge of a hillside, another historic Hill Country home was planned to be reconstructed—Alexander Auld's homestead, built near Leakey in the 1880s. Auld's son Dan, who happened to have been a friend of Ewing Halsell in the oil and cattle business, donated the house to the botanical garden in 1977. Dan's father "and a group of young Scotchmen" had cut pre–Ice Age piñon trees on a nearby hilltop, carried the logs down to the valley, and put them on oxcarts to reach the protective base of a three-hundred-foot cliff, where the fourteen-by-forty-seven-foot house had been built near a spring and a fern bank. It was considered the largest pioneer cabin of piñon logs in Texas. But estimates for moving and reconstructing the house ran upward of $65,000, more than $280,000 today.[121]

As the botanical garden's May 1980 opening day approached, expenses for other projects were already over budget and attention was focused elsewhere. The Schumacher house remained unassembled near its new site. Moving the Auld house would also have to wait for another day.

Young gardeners maintain their own raised beds as part of the Children's Vegetable Garden program, begun in 1983.

Launching the San Antonio Botanical Garden

For parks department workers charged with preparing the San Antonio Botanical Garden, opening the front door to visitors was like welcoming guests into a home while it was still being built. Some areas were planted sparsely or not at all. The Schumacher house lay un-reassembled in the Hill Country area, and the Auld house remained on its original site near Leakey, too costly to move. A conservatory, usually the hallmark of a botanical garden, was nowhere to be seen.

Nevertheless, at high noon on opening day—Saturday, May 3, 1980—the city's Parks and Recreation Department and the San Antonio Garden Center's botanical garden committee greeted the public at the garden's Fountain Plaza. Visitors stood in the shade of the gazebo on Observation Lookout and admired the skyline, explored paths through half a dozen new gardens, and enjoyed Greek, Czech, Polish, German, soul, and Hispanic cuisine and entertainment in the Texas Native area, its freshly planted young trees scarcely relieving the barrenness of the new site. As a bonus, visitors could walk next door to the annual flower show, themed "House Beautiful in Flowers," at the San Antonio Garden Center.[122]

How the garden would proceed depended on the parks department. The garden center's botanical garden committee, having completed the Garden for the Blind, considered its work done, and in response to feelers from the city rejected the idea of operating the garden. Gilbert Denman clearly saw that "for the garden to function as a real botanical garden, rather than merely as another city park," an independent, nonpolitical botanical society had to be formed and accept substantial responsibility.[123]

The botanical garden was dedicated at Fountain Plaza on May 3, 1980, with the plaque unveiling by Lucretia Murphy, forty years earlier one of the San Antonio Garden Center's two cofounders, and by parks and recreation director Ron Darner. The entrance was off Funston Place.

Taking the garden to a higher level would not be easy. Such a group would need to provide input to the parks department's search for a director, generate public support, raise funds for new development, negotiate policies with the city, and, for special events, find a way to remove Brackenridge's vexing ban on alcoholic beverage consumption in Mahncke Park.

Months before the opening, Denman had pitched his concept of an independent botanical society to parks department director Ron Darner, who suggested that the city might contract with the group "for certain operational functions and/or services." He assured Denman: "We have reached a point at which your organizational and managerial expertise can make a botanical society a reality. We are prepared to provide any needed administrative support."[124]

With that encouragement Denman tracked down Paul Weissich, director of the Honolulu Botanical Gardens, and used his contacts to identify and hire Bruce McAlpin, fern horticulturist at the New York Botanical Garden, as a consultant. Gathering thirty San Antonians to join him as trustees and directors, Denman succeeded in chartering the San Antonio Botanical Center Society by the end of the year, with Denman, Gretchen Northrup, and Margaret Deely as incorporators.[125]

Twenty-one directors attended the first quarterly board meeting in February 1981 at the botanical garden entry building. They elected Hall Hammond, recently active in forming the San Antonio Parks Council / Friends of the Parks, as president; civic leader Patsy Steves as vice president; businessman Louis P. Bishop as treasurer; and Robert Washington, the Ewing Halsell Foundation's grants coordinator, as secretary. The foundation contributed $10,000 to cover the botanical society's initial operating expenses. A ten-member executive committee would meet monthly.[126]

In April 1981 the society entered into a seven-page agreement with the city outlining the society's function as an auxiliary to the parks department supporting the botanical garden as "a publicly owned place of beauty for the benefit of the general public who visit the facility, a center for scientific research in the fields of botany and horticulture, and an educational and interpretive center in the fields of botany and horticulture."[127]

The city appropriated $75,000 to expand the entry building for office space and for the society's growing research library,

The original entrance building, on the future site of the Kelso Center, opened onto Fountain Plaza and provided space for meetings. A sketch of the doorway shows a window display in the garden's first gift shop.

The original one-room Schumacher house, built in Fredericksburg in 1849 of German half-timber construction, later gained a room built with post oaks and soon another with quarried limestone. The entire house was reconstructed at the garden in 1983.

begun with a collection of botanical reference books donated by Hall Hammond in 1982. The structure also housed a small gift shop operated by the city, until, in 1986, the botanical society purchased the inventory from the city at cost and was authorized to continue operations on its own. Elsewhere, work resumed on reconstructing the small 1849 Schumacher house, dedicated at a German-themed Gartenfest in mid-1983.[128]

Still on the horizon was constructing the four-room conservatory with a standing-seam metal roof. But botanical society leaders thought the garden deserved better. By the time the executive committee broached the topic in September 1981, Gibert Denman was already searching for a visionary architect to design a signature conservatory that would make a statement for the city, even if it cost well into the then unthinkable seven figures. The planning and construction process took on a life of its own.[129]

In April 1981 the city approved a new parks department position—botanical garden manager, commonly called director. This allowed a search for the position to begin. Six months later, Eric Tschanz, age thirty, was hired for the job. Denman had located Tschanz at the Cox Arboretum in Dayton, Ohio, where he was serving as superintendent of horticulture, and urged him to apply. Tschanz had a degree in horticulture from Ohio State University and a master's degree from the University of Delaware's Longwood Gardens program, which focused on public horticulture administration.[130]

Soon after his start in February 1982, Tschanz used new greenhouses in the maintenance area in the garden's northwest corner to house a collection of more than twenty rare cycads purchased at what he considered a bargain price. They also provided space for acquisitions from a cutting-edge plant collecting program, what Tschanz termed "a type of rescue-the-plants mission," to save native plants in areas scheduled for development. The developer of the Encino Park subdivision northeast of U.S. 281 and Loop 1604 gave permission for the first collecting foray. Some acquisitions were planted in the garden; others joined a plant distribution/exchange and sale. This broadened the initially formulated purposes of the botanical garden, an advance seen as helping the garden "rise to its place with other similar institutions."[131]

In 1982 Eric Tschanz became the botanical garden's first director.

By 1984 the garden had its first logo, a design of a plant and its roots.

By 2024 more than one hundred botanical society volunteers had rescued plants at more than eighty sites in the preceding few years. The volunteers were coordinated by the garden's education director, a position held from 1986 to 2003 by Betty Hughes, who also taught biology at San Antonio College.[132]

Viva Botanica featured springtime walks among food booths, demonstrations, and prize-winning exhibits, with Viva Navidad coming at Christmas. Pumpkin painting took advantage of the East Texas cabin's deep porch.

As an events schedule developed there were Shakespeare in the Park performances, docent-led horticultural tours, and seasonal events. In December 1981 the garden hosted a monthlong Viva Navidad with visiting choirs and Christmas lights strung throughout the garden. Viva Botanica weekend in spring 1983 featured food, music, horticulture displays, falconry demonstrations, and a performance by the San Antonio Symphony. It drew more than ten thousand visitors that year and later attracted some seventeen thousand. There were booths and exhibits by an array of conservation groups, demonstrations of pioneer crafts at the East Texas cabin, and a host of performances by dancers and entertainment groups.[133]

Another early success was the Children's Vegetable Garden at the botanical garden's eastern edge, beside Old Austin Road, where a white picket fence surrounded raised garden beds. Sponsored by the Men's Garden Club, the semiannual program of hands-on Saturday morning garden classes began in 1983 with participation by two dozen children between the ages of eight and twelve. On other days, students' assigned garden areas were maintained by adult volunteers. David Thomas, a recently retired brigadier general who had commanded Brooke Army Medical Center, ran the program for the first five years

David Thomas, who helped establish the Children's Vegetable Garden program in 1983, discusses a snake gourd with two young gardeners.

with the enthusiasm and gusto that could be expected of a Normandy paratrooper who had made a successful two-day escape after being captured by the Germans.[134]

"He valued the benefits of horse manure for organic compost," said Maverick Fisher, an alumnus of Thomas's first classes, "but warned that it would burn our plants unless it was allowed to age before using. He proved this to us by burying a carton of a dozen raw eggs one Saturday in a pile of manure from the Brackenridge Stables and extracting them a week later, soft-boiled."[135]

Participation grew and the age range was expanded to seven through sixteen. In spring 1992 enrollment reached its capacity of 121. Given the long waiting list, participants were limited to three seasons. Vegetable shows and harvest festivals were added.[136]

The garden began encouraging lower water use, not just its own but also the public's. In June 1985 four hundred people attended the dedication of Xeriscape, a half-acre demonstration garden at the edge of the maintenance area. The first of its kind in Texas, the garden offered ideas for low water use and sustainability. James Keeter designed its three garden areas, featuring more than one hundred types of low-water-tolerant plants selected in cooperation with the Edwards Underground Water District, the San Antonio River Authority, and the Bexar County Extension Service.[137]

During those years threats to the integrity of the botanical garden's site appeared from two unexpected projects.

In 1982 investor William Ochse Jr. planned a seventeen-story, sixty-four-unit condominium complex, Regency Gardens, on nearly two acres at the southeast corner of Funston Place and North New Braunfels Avenue. The luxury development would tower over the botanical garden. The botanical society joined forces with the three-year-old Mahncke Park Neighborhood Association to oppose it. The San Antonio Board of Adjustment delayed a decision on Ochse's request for zoning variances so he could sort things out with opponents. He did not manage to do so. At a hearing two months later, the society still took a strongly negative stance.[138]

In a written statement, society representatives asserted that "a structure of this immense height will ruin the aesthetic visual landscapes [and] would be a detriment to what has been and what is being created at the San Antonio Botanical Center." Therefore, the society was "adamantly opposed" to the project. Parks director Ronald Darner contributed a similar letter of opposition, noting that the garden's "panoramic view of the city is breathtaking" and that its "site characteristics far exceed those of most botanical gardens in the nation." Fifty members of the Mahncke Park Neighborhood Association appeared in person to oppose the project. The zoning board vote of 3–2 in favor of the project fell one short of the four votes needed to approve. Ochse made another try eight months later, but it also failed.[139]

Then, in 1985, oilman Walter S. Light proposed a ten-story, forty-five-unit condominium complex a block from the garden center, on North New Braunfels Avenue between Parland Place and Elmhurst Avenue. By that time Mahncke Park–area residents had developed a neighborhood plan in accordance with City Planning Department standards and had gotten it approved by the city council. The plan emphasized the area's residential character and opposed developments that would increase population density. For its part, the botanical society submitted a full-page resolution opposing all high-rise developments in the neighborhood and stressing the need to preserve its own "panoramic view of the city and verdant surroundings." The proposed development was not built.[140]

In January 1986 the garden's ten-member long-range planning committee, chaired by Gilbert Denman Jr., met in the offices of the Ewing Halsell Foundation to consider a dozen long-term goals. These included "the necessity of keeping the Garden as a learning institution and not merely another pleasant city park," developing a publications program, developing a new master plan, and expanding the garden into the thirteen acres of lower Mahncke Park as an arboretum, perhaps making "a serious educational impact by specializing in some type of trees, such as oaks."

There was already Freedom Grove, a copse of mixed trees and shrubs on the brink of the hillside west of North New Braunfels Avenue. Dedicated by the garden center for the nation's bicentennial in 1976 as an overlook for an arboretum, the grove was maintained by the botanical garden.[141]

Rex Moyer, a Trinity University biology professor and chair of the garden's Science and Education Committee, began work in 1987 on a thirty-one-page study for such an arboretum. It was seen as oriented toward scientific research and education, with a focus on trees and shrubs that grew well in San Antonio. An inventory the previous year had counted 405 trees in the lower section of Mahncke Park. Most common were mesquite (240), followed by cedar elm (88), live oak (8), pecan (7), and 62 additional species. Since a sizable number of dying trees were unlikely to be replaced by new growth, additional planting would be needed to maintain the sense of an urban forest.[142]

Moyer's study proposed concentrations of plantings at both ends of the arboretum, flanking an open area in the center. New plantings would include walnuts, chestnuts, palms, and persimmons. Along Broadway, the "stately mature live oaks and cedar elms" presented "a grand image for the arboretum." Improvements there would include new hardy elms and crape

Dedicating Freedom Grove in 1976 were (*from left*) garden center president Leta Baughn, San Antonio Conservation Society president Vivian Hamlin, Janey Briscoe (wife of Gov. Dolph Briscoe), and Mayor Lila Cockrell.

myrtle, a widened sidewalk, benches, and a display of the buried Spanish Alamo Madre acequia dug through in 1719.[143]

Curbside trees along Parland Place and Funston Place would provide a shaded canopy over the streets and create what Moyer saw as "an announcement and gateway" up to the botanical garden, where arboretum parking would be provided. The parks department would plant the trees and the botanical society would maintain them. To seek neighborhood cooperation, society representatives assured residents attending community forums that the arboretum would remain a neighborhood park. Garden staff began germinating palm seeds collected for the arboretum.[144]

Arboretum planning, however, sputtered. A $15,000 grant from the Marcia and Otto Koehler Foundation was used in 1987 to hire an Austin planning and landscape design firm to produce an arboretum master plan, but that process ended acrimoniously with an unfinished plan and a settlement in which the society diverted its final payment from the planning firm to pay one of the firm's consultants, who had not been paid.[145]

The botanical society shifted its focus to the move and reconstruction of an enormous stone carriage house, leaving a limited number of potential donors to tap for other projects. Any chance of arboretum funding from the city was seen as "years away." Denman promised that once the carriage house was finished arboretum plans "would be revisited," but that has yet to happen.[146]

A yellow-crowned night heron stands alert for a meal in the pond of Kumamoto En.

Kumamoto En and a Carriage House

With basic infrastructure in place and operations on an upswing, the botanical garden undertook two major projects in the late 1980s. The first was installing an authentic Japanese garden, which was completed in less than a year. The second was deconstructing, moving, and reassembling a spacious Victorian stone carriage house as the garden's new main entrance. The complicated effort took nearly eight years.

The Japanese garden stemmed from San Antonio's sister city relationship, begun in 1987, with Kumamoto, on Japan's southwestern island of Kyushu. It was an outgrowth of Mayor Henry Cisneros's efforts to bring Japanese industry to San Antonio and to promote San Antonio businesses in Japan. Cisneros hired Seiichi and Naoko Mitsui Shirane, members of aristocratic Japanese families, to establish the Texas–Japan Office in Tokyo.[147]

The sister cities commemorated their relationship with an exchange of gifts. San Antonio sent Kumamoto snow leopards from the San Antonio Zoo and a log cabin built in 1994 on botanical garden grounds and disassembled for shipment. Kumamoto reciprocated with materials and labor for the design and construction of Kumamoto En, or Kumamoto Garden, in the botanical garden. Kiyoshi Yasui, widely revered for his authentic temple reconstructions and nominated by the emperor of Japan as a national living treasure, designed the new garden.[148]

Yasui had his work cut out for him: creating the garden in a very small space and in an atypical environment. He had to do it in six months, a time frame, he noted, that "is unheard of in Japan." Though he sought inspiration from the three-hundred-year-old, thirteen-acre Suizenji Park in Kumamoto, the San Antonio site spanned less than a quarter acre. Yasui compressed thirty traditional Japanese

In 2000 revered Japanese architect Kiyoshi Yasui visited Kumamoto En, the garden he had designed eleven years earlier.

An *azumaya*, or tea waiting arbor, sits above left of the pond in the Japanese garden. One of the garden's four types of surrounding fences is in Daimyo/Shogun style, its chestnut posts holding bamboo branches sheared as a broomed top.

garden elements into an intense display of walks, water features, walls, and symbolic mountains.[149]

With no room for a customary teahouse, Yasui substituted a smaller tea waiting arbor, or *azumaya*, similar to one in Suizenji Park that he was allowed to copy due to his family's relationship with rulers of Japan. It was the first of its type in the United States. The Japanese crew that traveled to San Antonio made the roof out of hand-shaped copper strips. As in a true *azumaya*, its four benches were arranged to not face each other so that the eyes of those waiting for the tea ceremony would not meet and interrupt a time of introspection and meditation.[150]

"Mountains" were scaled down to berms, with one at the center representing Mount Fuji. A smaller berm on the western edge signified Mount Aso—the volcanic cauldron near Kumamoto—and another at the eastern edge symbolized an imaginary Mount San Antonio. A spring-fed stream flanked

San Antonio mayor Henry Cisneros tries on a traditional Japanese festival *happi* coat presented by Kumamoto mayor Norio Yoshida at the dedication of Kumamoto En in May 1989.

by junipers, ferns, and Japanese maples created waterfalls of different heights to produce varying sounds of falling water as it filled a pond representing the Pacific Ocean. Yasui individually selected four truckloads of stones in Japan and California, choosing those to be used to form the mountains from mountains, and those in water from water.

Yasui also picked the walkway stones—formal cut granite paving stones that would lead from the entrance, rounded stepping stones to slow visitors for meditation, smooth stones randomly mortared together for an even walking surface, and stepping stones to the water. These stones did not lead, however, through a traditional Japanese groundcover of mosses, which require cool temperatures and constant moisture. In consultation with local staff, Yasui selected *Zoysia tenuifolia*, a fine-bladed variety of Asian grass that could withstand the South Texas climate.[151]

Yasui said, without hesitation, that his favorite view of this realm of tranquility was "the view as you exit. When you are looking back you see the three-step waterfall, the trees, the other waterfalls, the mountains, and the pond."[152]

After Yasui blessed the location in a traditional Shinto ceremony, Parks and Recreation Department crews began site preparation in February 1989. Paul Cox, then in one of his stints as the botanical garden's interim director, recalled that laying out the project in advance was complicated, as information had to be exchanged with the architect in Japan by fax machine. One month later the renowned craftsman and landscaper Katsuoki Kawahara and a dozen skilled workers from across Japan arrived and construction began.[153]

As the dedication date neared, the Japanese crews worked "ten hours a day, six days a week," Cox said. They did take some time to explore their surroundings, however. "On their days off we took many field trips," he said, "to the zoo, on a picnic where we chased and caught an armadillo, went fishing, had several barbecues, played horseshoes [and] croquet." When bad weather delayed construction, botanical center workers "threw themselves into the action five to six at a time and often on weekends to help catch up." Kumamoto En was ready for the dedication on May 15.[154]

To ensure proper maintenance of the garden, in 1990 the City of Kumamoto hosted Cox in Japan for a six-week training course on the techniques of Japanese garden maintenance. More specialized maintenance would require visits by Japanese craftsmen every few years, particularly to replace the four distinctive bamboo perimeter fences.[155]

Yasui returned in summer 2000 to check on the garden for the first time since its dedication. "After eleven years I was very concerned about the garden," he said. "It is like a child. I haven't seen my child for eleven years, and I came back and he was good. I am very satisfied."[156]

A stream of other important Japanese visitors came to Kumamoto En during construction of a Toyota truck manufacturing plant in San Antonio. In 2005 Japan's ambassador to the United States paid a visit on his way to tour the manufacturing site. To fix wear and tear on the garden in time for those attending the plant's opening in 2006, the Toyota Foundation provided funds for the garden's restoration. Its rededication was attended by Kumamoto mayor Seishi Kohyama and more than twenty other officials from the city, including San Antonio mayor Phil Hardberger, and Naoko Shirane, who, with her late husband, had begun San Antonio's promotion in Japan. In April 2008 local Toyota CEO Kenji Fukuta joined 160 Toyota volunteers to clean Kumamoto En's pond—as well as its turtle made of stones, a surprise addition by the original Japanese workers as they finished the pond.[157]

The Japanese garden inspired a Day in Japan class at the garden in 1996.

As garden planning evolved in 2012, a proposal to relocate Kumamoto En closer to Funston Place was proposed by the botanical society and endorsed by former mayors Lila Cockrell and Henry Cisneros. Then came the realization that the initial Shinto blessing and rigid adherence to the nuances of Japanese design had made the garden a sacred Japanese site. When a "summit" meeting of the two sister cities was held in San Antonio in July 2013, a year short of Kumamoto En's twenty-fifth anniversary, the proposal had been dropped. The mayor of Kumamoto and eighteen others from there joined San Antonio officials in rededicating Kumamoto En at its original site.[158]

After the death of Naoko Shirane, the city commissioned San Antonio sculptor Donna L. Dobberfuhl to create a full-length statue of Shirane to be placed at Kumamoto En's entrance. Former mayor Henry Cisneros presided at the dedication in November 2016, and past Toyota chairman Shoichiro Toyoda made remarks.

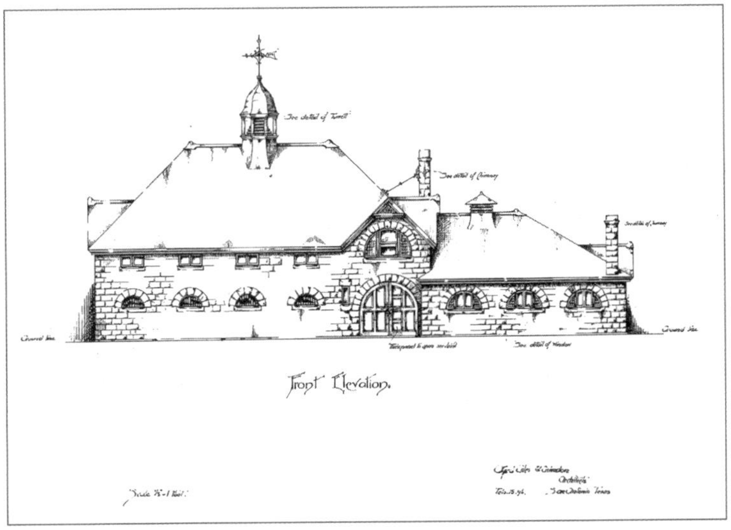

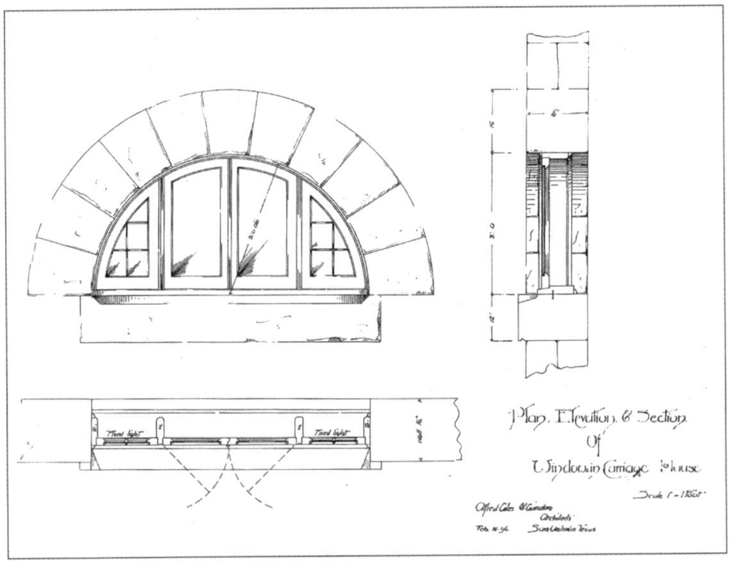

Banker Daniel Sullivan's elaborate 1896 carriage house is one of San Antonio's finest examples of Richardsonian Romanesque architecture.

Moving and reconstructing a landmark two-story stone carriage house three miles away to become the grand entrance to the San Antonio Botanical Garden was a quite different effort.

The carriage house was among San Antonio's finest examples of the uniquely American Richardsonian Romanesque architecture popular in the last two decades of the nineteenth century. The structure was designed in 1896 by a highly regarded local practitioner of that style, Alfred Giles, for Daniel J. Sullivan, an Irish-born private banker who made a fortune financing ranchers who sent their cattle up the Chisholm Trail. The carriage house stood behind Sullivan's home, razed in 1969, at the northeast corner of Broadway and Fourth Street. Its 4,400 square feet once held six carriages and eight horses plus glass-fronted harness and cleaning rooms at ground level. Upstairs were grooms' quarters and a hayloft with a chute to drop hay and grain into a machine at ground level for mixing feed.

The high quality of materials and workmanship boded well for the building's reuse. Giles used 1,200 blocks of ashlar limestone quarried near Kerrville to create a mix of semicircular masonry arches, hip roofs, cross gable rooflines, polygonal turrets, and simple arrangements of windows. Basic lumber was specified to be "best-picked" longleaf pine, the trim of white pine "free from all imperfections." The first floor was dirt, but upstairs flooring was to be the "best, no blue sap or knots, all laid face down in [a] most substantial manner, well-nailed at each joint and left perfect." For the galvanized standing seam tin roof, as with other elements, "no inferior work will be accepted."[159]

The carriage house became available when its owner, the *San Antonio Light*, said it could find no use for it other than a parking lot but was barred by a deed restriction from tearing it down. The building could, however, be moved off the property. The

The carriage house languished beside the *San Antonio Light* building and behind the parking lot on the Sullivan house site until 1987, when workers began numbering and disassembling its stones for reconstruction at the botanical garden.

Lowering of the original cupola into place in mid-1988 marked completion of the carriage house's basic reconstruction.

newspaper donated the structure to the San Antonio Museum Association, parent organization at the time of the Witte Museum, which hoped to reconstruct it on the site of the Witte's former alligator gardens. Then the museum association, unable to raise the funds, offered to sell an option on the carriage house to someone deemed able to carry out a viable plan for its moving and reconstruction. Various proposals fell through.[160]

Gilbert Denman Jr., chair of the botanical society's long-range planning committee, brought up the house to the society's executive committee in September 1986. Three weeks later society president Helen Hogan called a special meeting to consider taking on the project. Parks department director Ron Darner reported the city's willingness to accept ownership of the structure on its property and suggested that the society help fund a feasibility study proposed by the architectural firm Stubblefield-Mogas. That was approved, and Richard Mogas promptly prepared the study.[161]

Enthusiastic botanical society leaders optioned the carriage house. Robert Washington and then Helen Hogan led the fundraising effort. By September 1987 the society had raised $330,000, including $100,000 from the San Antonio Conservation Society Foundation and $50,000 from the Dallas-based Meadows Foundation. The San Antonio City Council passed an ordinance authorizing the project, with all costs to be borne by the society.[162]

In October 1987 cranes and forklifts assembled at the carriage house, scaffolding went up, and dismantling began. Doug Pape's Pape Construction Company removed roofing and interior floors and trusses, leaving the stone walls, photographed to show numbers marked on each stone to aid in precise reassembly. Masons under the direction of specialist Curtis Hunt carefully loosened mortar so stones could be separated without damage before being lowered, wrapped, and placed on pallets to be raised onto flatbed trucks for the journey.[163]

The carriage house was positioned on the most level ground at the edge of a slight grade just north of the garden's gatehouse. Its original orientation, southwest to northeast, was preserved to allow light to enter the building and cast shadows on the stones, as had been the case at the original location. Stones were placed, lumber elements reinstalled, the roof redecked, and door and window openings sealed with plywood to await interior restoration. The nearly one-ton octagonal cupola of yellow pine and cypress was hoisted over the roof and lowered into place on June 2, 1988, eight months after the deconstruction began.[164]

To celebrate, in October the botanical society held a black-tie dinner in the courtyard of the conservatory, completed eight months earlier. The dinner also recognized the successful carriage house efforts of the society's president, Helen Hogan, who received a historic preservation award from the president of the National Trust for Historic Preservation.[165]

Too, the fete launched fundraising efforts for some $500,000 of final carriage house work, to be overseen by Irby Hightower of Alamo Architects. Most of the carriage house's original elements needed only basic refurbishing, but much needed to be added—wiring, heating, cooling, plumbing, insulation, and dark gray slate floor tiles to evoke the original dirt ground floor. Larger questions lingered. A solution had to be found for drainage issues caused by construction and new paving, which sent runoff cascading into the Mahncke Park neighborhood below. Parking, ramps, landscaping, a courtyard, drainage, water lines, and handicapped access all delayed completion of the project until 1995.[166]

During the seven years since exterior reconstruction was completed, the carriage house remained closed, its doors and windows sealed with plywood. Finally nearby residents Jack and Laura Richmond, who lived in the high-rise 4001 Condominiums on North New Braunfels Avenue, asked their neighbor Edward Muir, an early botanical garden board member, why the stone building they could see from their balcony was kept boarded up. He alerted future botanical society president Cathy Garison, and before long the Richmonds wrote a check that got the project moving again.[167]

Also resolved during that time was the operational issue over whether the structure should be configured as the entrance to the garden, as the exit, or as both. Ultimately the society decided that visitors would enter the garden from the parking

A patio planted with trees went behind the rebuilt carriage house, and onetime horse stalls indoors became booths for diners in the restaurant.

lot through the carriage house's west door and walk straight to the eastern door into a newly excavated courtyard. Visitors would leave the garden by reentering the eastern door and turning left down a hall to the southern door, passing the newly relocated Garden Gate Gift Shop in former carriage storage space. The grooms' quarters upstairs would become a lecture hall and meeting room featuring an early Texas table donated by the Alamo Heights–Terrell Hills Garden Club.[168]

The Carriage House Kitchen, an 1,800-square-foot restaurant space with seating for up to eighty, would occupy the north end of the ground level. Eight horse stalls with decorative ironwork were converted to booths, and double

Restoration was finished in 1995, and the carriage house became the gateway to the garden.

stalls for mares and foals were converted to a small kitchen. The restaurant space would go through challenges of its own after the entrance eventually opened. After a series of lessees struggled with menus and operating hours, in 2007 the Sullivan Family Charitable Foundation would cover two-thirds of a $300,000 code compliance upgrade to a commercial kitchen to attract a more established lessee. The botanical society would select San Antonio's RK Group, known nationwide for culinary and hospitality services. Later lessees would include chef Jason Dady, who began a five-year tenure in 2020. After that, with funding by the Daniel J. Sullivan Family Charitable Foundation, the restaurant would be converted to rental space for special events and the upstairs to office space.[169]

Back in June 1994, final site development for the carriage house was just beginning. Carriage house committee chair and former society president Margaret Deely donned a hard hat and climbed onto a bulldozer to kick off the ceremony, presided over by society president Robert Downey.

A year later, on Saturday, June 17, 1995, a Picnic and Parade Day celebrated completion of the project. Celebrants, including members of the Sullivan and Giles families, gathered at the conservatory courtyard to "walk, skip, march or dance" in a parade to the carriage house with wheelbarrows, tricycles, wagons, or baby carriages. Former mayor Lila Cockrell presided over a ribbon cutting and tree planting.[170]

When Deely celebrated her one hundredth birthday in the carriage house restaurant in June 2009, the giant century plant outside the carriage house's front door was in full bloom.[171]

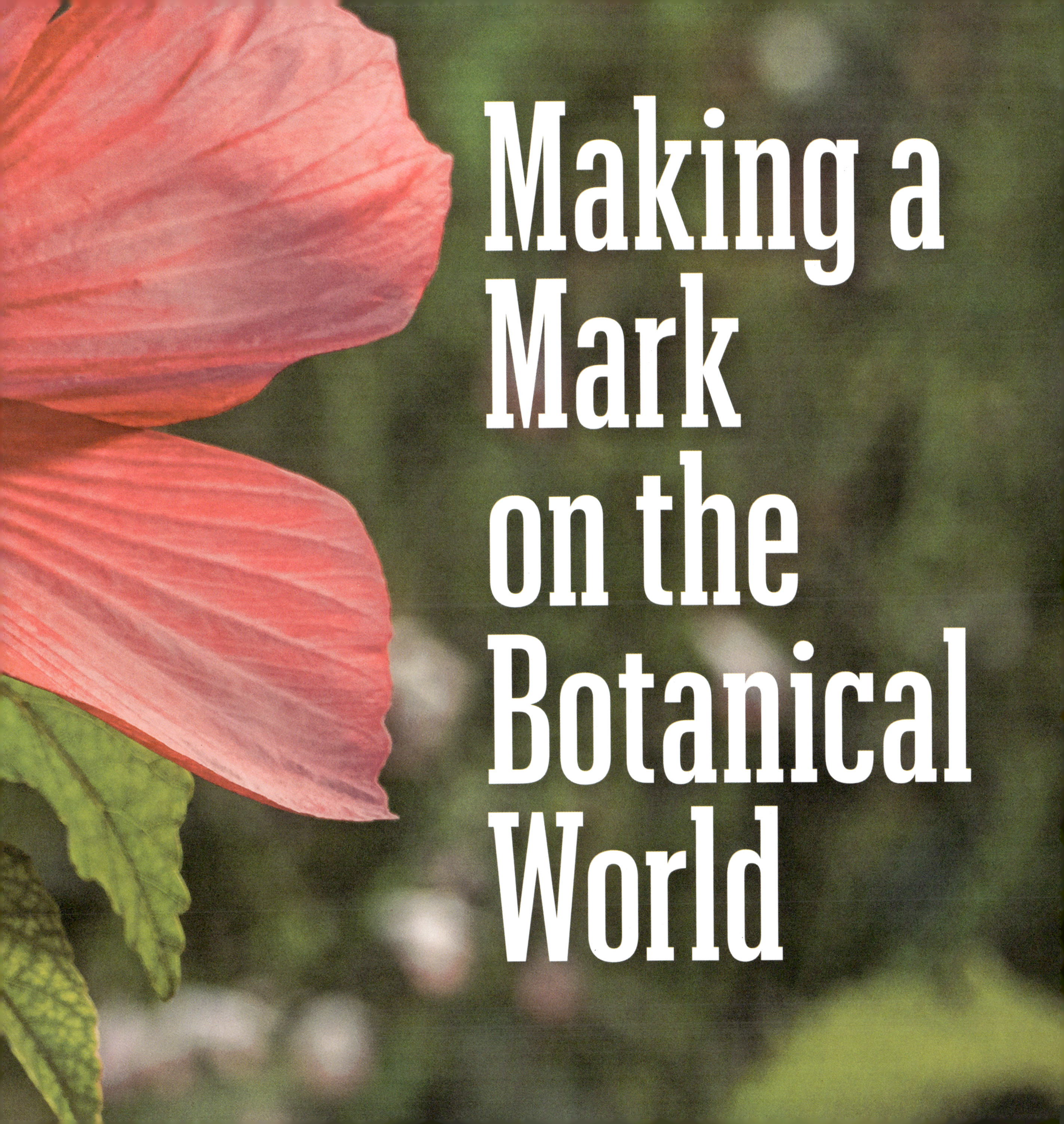

Making a Mark on the Botanical World

The Moy Grande, thought to be the largest open-faced garden flower in the world, was developed by Ying Doon Moy.

The Moy Grande Leads the Way

Ying Doon Moy was correctly addressed as Mr. Ying, not Mr. Moy. "He tried in vain to explain that in Chinese the names are reversed and that his more proper title would be 'Mr. Ying,'" longtime staff member Paul Cox said of the botanical garden's legendary horticulturist and geneticist. But "after years of trying to correct us," he finally realized "we were untrainable" and accepted Mr. Moy.[172]

By whatever name, the Chinese refugee brought international renown to the San Antonio Botanical Garden for his development of the Moy Grande, a hibiscus hybrid that is considered the largest open-faced flower in the world. He also brought regional renown for hybridizing papayas and other plants to make them suitable for the South Texas climate. The garden has had other notable triumphs in its ongoing programs of plant conservation and development, but the story of Mr. Moy and his work is without compare.

Ying Doon Moy was born in 1929 in a village near Hong Kong. At age eleven he decided his future was in horticulture. He remembered his grandmother growing vegetables and flowers, but he found inspiration for his career choice elsewhere. "There was a beautiful flower shop in Kowloon, and I loved to go there," he recalled. "I was impressed by the flowers' beauty, size, color, and smell."

Moy did his undergraduate and graduate studies in Canton (now Guangzhou) at the Agricultural University of South China, which granted him a doctoral degree and named him associate professor in charge of genetic research on citrus and vegetables. While there he successfully developed seedless watermelons, improved the sweetness of pineapples and lychee, and trained many other plant geneticists. Several Asian citrus varieties and a pineapple were named in his honor. He survived World War II but was stripped of his title during the Cultural Revolution that began two decades later. The Communist Chinese government forced him into a program of hard labor, and livestock turned loose in his test

Ying Doon Moy holds an award-winning type of papaya he developed at the botanical garden.

planting areas destroyed his prized crosses of plants not in the same genus. He escaped with his wife and two sons. They hid in caves and survived on weeds, the cause of his lifelong dislike for purslane, according to one associate.

The family managed to flee China and join relatives in Chicago, though Moy found the cold climate unsuitable for continuing his research in subtropical plants. In 1980 they moved to San Antonio, where his brother-in-law lived and where the warmer climate was much like Guangzhou's. Moy started a job search by applying for the position of city agronomist. Paul Cox, then working in the parks department office while also managing the botanical garden, interviewed him.[173]

Slight of stature, immaculately dressed, and self-effacing while still maintaining a dignified bearing, Moy kept a perpetual smile on his lips. His distinguished demeanor impressed Cox, as did Moy's enthusiasm and sincerity. Cox explained that the job mainly involved seeding and fertilizing turf on city parks' playing fields. Moy asked for a job at the new botanical garden instead. He was highly overqualified for the only opening, for a gardener, but took it anyway.

For that job, however, he was sent instead to the city nursery in Brackenridge Park. Not fluent in English, Moy endured some discrimination, Cox said, but stuck it out and became recognized for a strong work ethic.

Cox soon helped Moy get a transfer to the botanical garden, where Cox said he was "always addressed as Mr. or Dr. as a gesture of respect." Moy was eventually promoted to horticulturist in charge of the main color beds, Rose Garden, Sacred Garden, and Garden for the Blind, later renamed the Sensory Garden. Cox said Moy would target the date of the annual Viva Botanica weekend to have the roses in full bloom and missed the date only once.

"When I asked him why his plants were always healthier than anyone else's," Cox recalled, "he replied that he talked to his plants," meaning that he "simply had the experienced eye that could discern the plants' cultural needs." He also planted according to phases of the moon. Longtime volunteer Harry Mazal saw Moy as walking through his gardens "with the firm steps of a benevolent creator, ever pinching off an errant bud or arranging compost around the trunk so that it looked just so, talking to his plants as if they could (and probably do) understand his love for nature and their beauty."[174]

Moy faced a larger challenge in hybridizing plants grown in cooler climates to make them more suitable for South Texas. He could be difficult to understand because of his Chinese accent, said San Antonio–based Texas A&M University horticulturist

Jerry Parsons, but "local horticulturists had no problem conveying to him the needs for plant improvement to increase marketability and survivability in arid southwest Texas."[175]

Moy's impact on the botanical garden was even more impressive because he had no assistants and performed all crossings, collection and cleaning of seeds, planting, and care himself. He developed more than 150 species and other hybrids of papaya; fifty-seven varieties of hibiscus; and various hybrids of ginger, roses, and esperanza. He also played a key role in adapting the subtropical papaya to the local climate. In the early days of the botanical garden, horticulturists and gardeners planted papayas for their displays of showy tropical fruit, even though they took fifteen months to mature and did not survive the usual winter freeze. But after a few years staff noticed that some papaya plants were getting shorter and bearing mature fruits in a single season. Moy revealed that he was crossing the plants to produce large, early fruit. But the resulting fruit was relatively tasteless.

With staff encouragement, Moy began crossing a Mexican yellow papaya with the more sugary Hawaiian Solo and developing the San Antonio Sweet and the San Antonio Early. But the only way he could test the flavor was to get the staff to eat them. Because each plant yielded up to 130 pounds of fruit a season, Cox said the "staff began to run away when they saw Moy approaching with papayas in hand." Parsons, whom Moy considered his "number one friend," provided a sugar refractometer so Moy could do scientific testing himself.[176]

The resulting papayas became the garden's signature plant, won Moy his first awards in the United States, and generated significant revenue for the garden through the society's volunteer plant sales group, which raised funds by selling exotic and unusual plants not found at local nurseries. For the spring 1997 Viva Botanica, sixteen volunteers and Master Gardeners worked daily to raise more than fifteen hundred papaya plants, all of which sold at $14 each. With hundreds of mature papayas also selling out at fall events, volunteer Harry Mazal, sales group cochair with Marjie Scharff, reported that overall sales in two years had raised more than $40,000. These proceeds were used to build a fully equipped six-thousand-square-foot greenhouse for "Mr. Moy's Magic Garden." Mazal also engineered the donation from Zachry Construction of a mobile office trailer to serve as Moy's office.[177]

A giant hibiscus named Moy Grande gained him the greatest acclaim. The hibiscus belongs to the mallow family in a genus known as perennial hibiscus or rose-mallow hibiscus. Flowers provide a continuous display of summer color, making them a popular plant for flower gardeners.

The image for the garden's new logo was the Moy Grande, its irregular petal edges adapted by designer Bradford Lawton as outlines of the Alamo.

"I actually had a hand in his most famous production," wrote Greg Grant, a horticulturist at the botanical garden at the time. Moy was breeding hibiscus hybrids to produce smaller, more weather tolerant blooms. He showed Grant the seedling crosses. "I couldn't help but notice a giant among them," Grant recalled. "When I told him how impressive it was, he explained how it was too big."[178]

Moy had crossbred the hybrid *Hibiscus moscheuto* ("Southern Belle"), which usually produces eight-inch blooms, with *Hibiscus grandiflora*, which produces ten-inch blooms. The resulting Moy Grande, considered superior to both parents, produced rose-pink blooms of twelve to fourteen inches. Grant called Parsons over to take a look. Parsons took cuttings back to a nursery and rooted them. "And without one peep of Mr. Moy's permission, we proceeded to both name and introduce his behemoth creation."[179]

In 2004 the Moy Grande became the new logo for the botanical garden. Veteran designer Bradford Lawton incorporated the Alamo motif at the end of each of the five petals,

Sara Eyestone, artist for the garden poster celebrating the Moy Grande hibiscus, signs a copy at Viva Botanica in 2000 as Sara Higginson looks on.

and it became one of his favorite designs. "It was a rebellious response to another designer who told me that no designer worth anything would ever use the Alamo," he recalled.[180]

But the Moy Grande, thought to be the largest open-faced garden flower in the world and soon a finalist for the Garden Club of America's Freeman Medal, was not patented. A year before the Moy Grande was developed, the garden had abandoned the idea of patenting new varieties as a "lengthy

Ying Doon Moy stops beside a bougainvillea tree to chat with volunteer Wayne Hand at Viva Botanica in 2003.

and awkward" process. Director Eric Lautzenheiser informed society board members that new varieties would be free "to any commercial company who wants them and will work with Jerry Parsons and the Texas Department of Agriculture." In addition to avoiding paperwork, this approach would create "good will with the industry." Thus the Moy was released for unrestricted sales in mid-1995 and soon spread around the world. One Texas horticulturist spotted the variety at a nursery in the coastal mountains of Ninghai, China.[181]

Another of Moy's triumphs was the Hedychium "Dr. Moy," termed "a true breakthrough" as the first variegated foliage winter-hardy ginger lily and rated best-of-class by London's Royal Botanic Gardens, Kew. Its four-inch stalks are topped by peachy-orange flowers.[182]

Ying Doon Moy retired as research director at the botanical garden in January 1999 after a career of eighteen years. Two years before he left, he and Jerry Parsons were the first to successfully cross the winter-hardy Changsha tangerine with the

Satsuma, noted for its fruit quality. They had carefully removed the Changsha flower anthers—the parts of the stamen producing the pollen. They applied the extracted Satsuma pollen and nurtured the sexually produced embryo from the Changsha seed. Seedlings were planted in containers to develop and mature for seven years.

Moy returned in 2004 to monitor progress of the Changsha-Satsuma seedlings and stayed for four years as a part-time plant researcher and consultant, developing more than fifty new hybrids of gingers, pomegranates, papayas, and citrus. Moy, with Parsons and Larry Stein of the Texas A&M Extension Service in Uvalde, rooted cuttings from the seedlings and planted them in ten-gallon containers for trial plantings outdoors, a phase several years away. Since Moy would not be there by that time, the botanical garden sold the collection and rights to an East Texas nursery for final evaluation and development. The nursery successfully released the resulting cold-hardy Orange Frost Satsuma, and in 2014 it was awarded a Texas Superstar designation by Texas A&M University.[183]

Ever the gentleman, at the close of his final San Antonio research report, written in January 2008, Moy thanked those who had helped him: Candace Andrews, managing director of the botanical society, who "always gives encouragement and support to finish the annual report," and horticulturist Scott Litchke and Robert Reed, "who always offer friendly support to finish the hard job any time work is needed to finish in the research garden."

Moy continued: "At last I deeply thank to all of the staffs of the San Antonio Botanical Garden and San Antonio Botanical Society for their friendship and support. I never forget that, they are deeply preserved in my heart."[184]

In 2008 Ying Doon Moy rejoined his family in Spring, north of Houston, and spent time nearby in research and development at the Mercer Arboretum, where he worked on breeding vegetation that would thrive in the Houston area's challenging climate. He died in August 2012 at the age of eighty-three. His family asked for a copy of the garden's Moy Grande hibiscus logo to put on his gravestone.[185]

Patty Leslie Pasztor, shown examining fourwing saltbush, was the garden's first native areas horticulturist and helped the garden become a founding member of the Center for Plant Conservation.

During Moy's tenure at the botanical garden, others also worked in plant development and conservation, "scientific, educational, and aesthetic aspects" mandated as fundamental in the botanical society bylaws. One of the first committees the society organized was its Science and Education Committee. Delbert Weniger, veteran Our Lady of the Lake University biology professor, Texas naturalist, and author of two books on cacti, served as its initial chair. His committee determined that after growing, exhibiting, and propagating Texas native and exotic plants, the garden's next priority should be "propagation of plants for distribution of rare and useful species."[186]

In 1984 the U.S. Fish and Wildlife Service's Center for Plant Conservation, based in San Diego, selected the botanical garden as one of the seventeen founding botanical gardens in the United States. All would participate in gathering a national

In 1987 the garden began reintroducing the Texas snowbell in the Hill Country.

The endangered Walker's manihot was added to the garden's collection in 1988.

collection of rare and endangered plants and to build up seed banks, in particular at the National Seed Storage Laboratory in Fort Collins, Colorado. They were also to host and research propagation and growing protocols for endangered plants. The garden's selection is attributed to the "enthusiasm and energy" of Patty Leslie Pasztor, the garden's first native areas horticulturist, a post she held for nearly ten years. The designation encouraged grants to the botanical garden like one for $14,700 to study a rare orchid quaintly named Navasota ladies' tresses (*Spiranthes parksii*) and an imperiled hardy Hill Country shrub, the Texas snowbell (*Styrax platanifolius* ssp. *texanus*), which can grow up to ten feet on the faces of rock cliffs and produces a springtime profusion of half-inch, bell-shaped white flowers favored by bees.[187]

In 1987 the U.S. Fish and Wildlife Service commissioned the garden to begin a long-term program to reintroduce the Texas snowbell in the Hill Country. Program leader Toney Keeny, professor of botany at what is now Southwest Texas College in Uvalde, oversaw workers who clung to ladders leaning against cliffs at two different sites to plant fifty Texas snowbells and add cages to protect them from animals. Two weeks of heavy rains destroyed more than a dozen, but new plantings in safer locations grew so well that by the next season they needed larger cages.[188]

A check twelve years later found that half of the plants had survived. At the first site, nine had grown to a height of five feet. At the second, a herd of wild goats had kept the thirteen survivors from growing beyond their cages. Nevertheless, said

Paul Cox, "it is a tribute to the tenacity of the species that so many were still alive."[189]

Cox, an early supporter of rare plant conservation at the garden, also developed the Bubba variety of desert willow (*Chilopsis linearis*). The vigorous, drought-tolerant, fast-growing shrub or small tree with dark burgundy and pink blossoms has become a favorite for landscapes throughout the Southwest.

The garden's Center for Plant Conservation collection has grown to more than twenty rare Texas specimens, among them the Anacacho orchid tree (*Bauhinia lunarioides*), nodding yucca (*Yucca cernua*), and Trans-Pecos milkvine (*Matelea texensis*). In addition the garden has collected plants or seeds of more than a hundred at-risk types of Texas plants. The largest concentration can be found in the Rare and Endangered Garden, five thousand square feet of planted beds and trails between the Children's Vegetable Garden and the South Texas trail.[190]

In 1988, two rare examples of Walker's manihot (*Manihot walkerae*) were added to the collection. Not only is Walker's manihot endangered, the species may have a practical use: The plant with five-lobed flowers may carry disease-resistant genes.[191]

The potential for conducting medical research using the garden's plants was pursued by Susan Mooberry, associate scientist at what is now the Texas Biomedical Research Institute and a chair of the garden's Science and Education Committee. In 2005 the garden grew Tacca plants, also known as batflowers, which contain compounds that Mooberry's studies indicated might feature anticancer properties. "They were not easy to grow," she said, "so this was a big deal." Mooberry and her team also collected 121 other native Texas species at the garden for cancer research. Though they isolated several previously unknown compounds from the Tacca and other plants, which led to publication of the results in professional journals, the compounds' properties were deemed not optimal for clinical development.[192]

Certified American Honey Show judge Monica Siwiak with garden advisory board member Robert Holliday, president of the Alamo Area Beekeepers Association, at a judging of area honey at the garden.

The botanical garden has increased plant conservation efforts as some 240,000 acres are being developed annually in Texas, equaling an area the size of Big Bend National Park every three and a half years. Eight native Texas plant species have gone extinct in the past hundred years. In addition to preservation work with the Center for Plant Conservation, the garden established its own Texas seed bank to include such short-lived aquatic plants as the Mexican mud-plantain (*Heteranthera mexicana*). Though the garden's conservation seed collections were once limited to short-term storage—for up to five years—they can now be stored for decades. Orchid seeds collected in Texas are sent to Longwood Gardens in Pennsylvania and the Huntington in California for propagation and return.[193]

Collected seeds that must germinate in one season, such as the acorns of oak trees, are germinated and grown until large enough to be planted, explained Michael Eason, associate director of conservation and collections at the botanical garden since 2017. Graftings or cuttings are made for propagating oaks when their acorns cannot be collected. The garden holds more than 120 of the some 500 types of oaks worldwide. The majority of these are in the greenhouse area and near the new WaterSaver Community exhibit, an area where so many oak trees were planted in the earliest days of the garden that staff members named it the Oaketum—a place for oaks.[194]

Michael Eason (*above, fourth from left*), part of a nine-member search team, found a Chisos Mountains oak, believed extinct, at Big Bend National Park. He later nurtured its seedlings (*right*) at the garden.

Aiding pollination in the garden were bees in a cluster of hives set up near the WaterSaver Community with the aid of advisory board member Robert Holliday, who served as president of the Alamo Area Beekeepers Association. It became the demonstration site for an Introduction to Urban Beekeeping class.

Amid tasks of preservation and experimentation came moments of complete surprise.

A Big Red Sage (*Salvia pentstemonoides*), a five-foot perennial in the mint family once common to central Hill Country creek banks and seep areas but thought to have been extinct since the 1930s, was found in 1987. Its seeds, taken to the botanical garden, had a germination rate of nearly 100 percent.[195]

Michael Eason made a similar discovery in 2022. He participated in a nine-member search team in Big Bend

The garden's seed bank includes seeds from a rare many-flowered devil's claw and those gathered from a bald cypress by conservation tech Cory Foshee.

National Park led by the Morton Arboretum and the United States Botanic Garden to look for the Chisos Mountains oak (*Quercus tardifolia*), first identified in 1930 but believed to have gone extinct in 2011.

"It was like when folks go searching for a lost child in the woods," Eason said, describing how team members spaced themselves a hundred feet apart in a line and combed through numerous areas. On the third day he found himself in front of a thirty-foot-tall specimen of the oak in Big Bend's Boot Canyon. Once he saw the short, matted hairs on the underside of a leaf, he recalled, "I knew this was it."[196]

The oak was in poor condition, with fire damage and a possible fungal infection. Team members planned to return in the winter to take samples for propagating the tree and to eventually reintroduce it to the wild. In the meantime, cuttings from the Chisos Mountains oak produced numerous seedlings in a botanical garden greenhouse.

Two years later, in 2024, Eason was driving through Jeff Davis County in West Texas "patrolling roadsides" for distinctive plants when he noticed a "very unusual" variety of devil's claw, the native southwestern plant known for its distinctive hooked seedpods. He observed that, unlike other types, these flowers were held well above the leaves on spikes and the plant was much smaller, as were the flowers, about half the size of the common fragrant devil's claw, which can grow as tall as two feet.

The plant he found was the rare *Proboscidea spicata*, or many-flowered devil's claw, a variety last documented several decades earlier and considered possibly extinct by the Center for Plant Conservation. Eason found a similar plant four feet away but, for miles in either direction, no others.

When he checked on them a month later they had been mown down. Their remaining fruit was not yet fully developed. Eason said he was "heartbroken."

Early the next fall, after a season of ample rains, he returned to the site. There stood more of the plants, one bearing mature fruit. Eason collected the fruit and brought it back to the garden. Some seeds would be planted to see if the new plants remained the same size as their predecessors in the wild or whether their size was determined by environmental conditions. Other seeds would be added to the garden's seed bank and, at the organization's request, to the national seed bank of the Center for Plant Conservation.[197]

Funston Place still curved past the conservatory to join Old Austin Road when this photo was taken from the SeaWorld blimp by board member Mary M. Fisher in 1993.

Paul Cox shows the impact point on a pane shattered by vandals at the conservatory.

Complications and Renewal

Architectural drama, shaded trails, flowering gardens, and botanical innovation may have transformed a desolate ridge into the San Antonio Botanical Garden, but lurking impediments to its future growth required imagination, patience, and dollars to resolve over the next decades.

Hostile fire from across a border presented one barrier to advancement. As soon as Emilio Ambasz's conservatory of towering glass cones opened in 1988, miscreants along Funston Place beside it targeted its immense panes of glass with rocks and pellet guns. The broken panes, as large as four feet by eight feet, cost at least $1,000 each, plus installation. Damages totaled $40,000—some $100,000 today—in just two years.[198]

Then there was neighborhood decline. What started as a series of two-story multiunit homes built by developers on the far side of Funston Place during World War II to accommodate those wanting to live near Fort Sam Houston had, often under absentee ownership, declined precipitously over time. By the 1980s city councilman Weir Labatt termed the crime-ridden area a haven for drug traffickers. One resident complained that he was robbed three times in three years.[199]

Garden leaders decided to solve the issue by purchasing the dilapidated structures—of which there were twenty-nine—and getting the city to close that section of Funston Place, creating a buffer zone to protect the conservatory. This approach also offered the significant benefit of adding eight acres to the garden, increasing its area by 25 percent. But it took nearly twenty years to complete the project. In the meantime, the question of when or if all the purchases could be accomplished loomed over future growth, for any master planning process required certainty.[200]

The botanical society got off to a good start on the Funston project. At the end of 1989, a year after the conservatory opened, the society used a $300,000 grant from the Ewing Halsell Foundation to purchase twelve of the Funston houses.

Twenty-six aging multiunit Funston Place homes across from the garden had been purchased and demolished by 1994.

As required, ownership of the properties was transferred to the city, the garden's landlord. Gilbert Denman Jr. reported that his long-range planning committee's primary goal was to purchase all seventeen remaining houses so the entire street could be closed and the land added to the garden. Parks and recreation director Ron Darner was less ambitious, saying that negotiations were to buy just eight of the seventeen remaining houses to create a smaller buffer zone and that the city would not close the street.[201]

Once the city purchased those eight houses, Denman overcame the city's hesitation to purchase the remaining nine with the promise that the Ewing Halsell Foundation would foot the bill, though costs did not end with the purchase; dealing with asbestos shingles sharply increased the expense of demolition. In addition, as more houses were purchased, remaining owners imposed demands not limited to higher sales prices. One owner requested compensation for lost future rent plus $2,750 in stipends to pay current tenants for premature termination of their leases. Other owners would settle for less. One requested four hours of free landscape consultation on her own home (she received a $300 voucher), and another simply wanted a five-year family membership to the garden. The Ewing Halsell Foundation funded purchase of six more houses in 1994, but negotiations for the remaining three slowed nearly to a halt. Ten years later two properties were still left, and the street remained open.[202]

Despite concern over the need for a master plan, the uncertainty of when and how the new Funston Place property should be dealt with influenced suspension of master planning efforts in 1996. Following completion of the conservatory, in 1989 a committee chaired by board member John Troy had begun a planning process that paused twice to absorb the unforeseen addition of Kumamoto En and of the Sullivan Carriage House. But the conceptual plan finally presented to the executive committee in June 1996 was tabled. The society's master planning efforts did not resume until the issue of the Funston properties was resolved twelve years later. In 1999 the Parks and Recreation Department tried doing a master plan on its own. Proposals included construction between the original entry building and the carriage house of a three-story education building, instead of the "garden party sun house" proposed in the earlier concept. But the parks department's plan was also not put into effect.[203]

In the meantime, the botanical society was overcoming several fundamental challenges. One dated back to George Brackenridge's donation of Mahncke Park. Another related to the current operational control of the garden by the city and the difficulties this presented when hiring and retaining directors. A major attraction—the Texas Native Area—also required special attention.

The historical issue was the restriction Brackenridge had included in his 1905 deed gifting Mahncke Park to the city as he had in his earlier gift of Brackenridge Park: that no alcoholic beverages could be consumed in the park. If that restriction were violated, ownership of the park would immediately transfer to the state of Texas for the benefit of the University of Texas. The Brackenridge Park Golf Course was dealing with the same issue. In 1985 the city persuaded the Texas Legislature to pass House Bill 1235, permitting the University of Texas board of regents to sell or convey its reversionary interest in both the golf course and botanical garden tracts to the city of San Antonio "for a consideration the board considers appropriate."[204]

In 1998 Mayor Howard Peak, garden officials, and Auld family members gathered in the Hill Country section of the Texas Native area for groundbreaking of the Auld house reconstruction. Logs disassembled at the original site near Leakey were laid out around the new slab and reassembled.

Mayor Phil Hardberger cuts a "vine" with pruning shears to open the enhanced Texas Native Trail area in 2006 while botanical society president Cathy Garison (*far right*) and others look on.

Although UT regents did not initially accept an agreement with either the botanical garden or the golf course, they had permitted drinks at public or private fundraising events held after regular hours. When UT reimposed the total ban in 1997, society attorney and past president Pat Deely reapproached the city, which proposed surrendering rights it had to purchase six acres of state-owned land on HemisFair Plaza next to the University of Texas's Institute of Texan Cultures if the state would surrender its contingent right to ownership of Mahncke Park. Regents rejected the offer but finally released their rights on the botanical garden site in 1998.[205]

Meanwhile the botanical society prepared to finish some business in the Texas Native Area, where since 1977 a site had been kept open for the 1880s Auld house, built near Leakey and donated to the garden by Dan Auld but then deemed too expensive to move and restore. Twenty years later the society marshaled the resources to dismantle the cabin and move its components to the garden, aided by board member and cabin restoration aficionado Cecil Jackson and with board president Wally McGee as project chair.[206]

With six grants and other gifts totaling some $100,000 in hand, groundbreaking ceremonies went forward in mid-1998 featuring Mayor Howard Peak and Auld family members. Chief architect was Ken Rehler of Rehler, Vaughn, and Koone. Bartlett Cocke Inc. was the general contractor. When reassembly and restoration ended two years later the cabin had air-conditioned meeting space for up to forty people and a new pavilion at the rear with adjacent restrooms, a storage room, and a small kitchen for caterers. The stucco exterior was not replaced to allow the underlying hand-cut logs to be visible.[207]

With that project at last complete, the botanical society addressed the need for better definition and interpretive signage for the eleven acres evoking the Hill Country, East Texas Pineywoods, and South Texas Plains. The area's trail system was made confusing by several entry and exit points and service road crossings. One trailside visitor was asked whether he had ever visited the native plants area. He replied that he had not. He was standing in the heart of that area.[208]

To address these problems, a new central kiosk was designed as a hub for trails to the three Texas areas individually and for a route looping through them all. Along the Hill Country trail, a wildflower meadow was added near a faux spring seeping from a new limestone bluff. The improvements were designed by landscape architect Jon S. Emerson of Baton Rouge, Louisiana, working with Sarah Lake and John Troy, landscape architects, board members, and project cochairs for the society. Troy, later a society president, in 1987 had begun the first of his board terms that led to a record of thirty years as a voting board member. The society president at the time, Cathy Garison, hosted Mayor Phil Hardberger at the grand opening of the Texas Native Trail, renamed from the Texas Native Area, in April 2006, a weekend event that drew three thousand visitors.[209]

Next came attention to the Texas Native Trail's focal point, the East Texas lake. Thirty years of sediment had shrunk the lake's depth to between thirteen and eighteen inches. Cattails flourishing in the shallow water overran the pond. This was a plus for the Kickapoo Traditional Tribe of Texas, recalled

Re-dredged in 2007, the East Texas lake kept its appeal for those enjoying a view or on a stroll.

Viewers at the Lende Bird Watch structure are invisible through the one-way glass to birds on the other side.

longtime garden staff member Scott Litchke, as tribal members from their reservation near Eagle Pass reaped armloads of the cattails for use in tribal ceremonies. To restore the depth to six to nine feet, Zachry Construction crews spent six weeks in mid-2007 dredging the lake, removing 3,700 cubic yards of silt that were hauled off in 246 truckloads. The bottom was resealed with 44 tons of bentonite, an absorbent clay. A wooden observation deck was built out from the shore over part of the lake.[210]

Just south of the lake, in a 2010 project funded by Bill, Bob, and Elizabeth Lende, architect Graham Martin designed a bird watch shelter resembling a South Texas cattle holding pen, with large panes of one-way glass so viewers inside could observe birds in the nearby brush without being seen by the birds. Plantings were selected to attract birds throughout the year. A rain-collecting cistern and trough provided water for birds to drink and splash.[211]

In addition to completing specific projects like these, the botanical society was expanding its organization and staff. In 1996 it increased its fundraising capacity by hiring a development director, Gloria Duke-Richter, as its first full-time

A spot where water seeps through limestone along the Hill Country trail was named for Candace Andrews, who coordinated with the parks department as the botanical society's managing director for eleven years.

Paul Cox steps into a cart loaded with a bois d'arc sapling being planted in 1983 by William Fisher (*right*) in one of some two dozen Eagle Scout projects Cox oversaw at the garden.

employee. When she resigned two years later, the society hired Candace Andrews, a board member for the previous seven years, and gave her the broader title of managing director. In 2000 the society added a full-time assistant to handle events. Later this assistant began overseeing rental of garden facilities, a process previously handled by the parks department but turned over to the society in 2002. By 2006 the society was working with its own operating budget of $1.5 million; its full-time staff had risen to four.[212]

Though the society and the parks department had a positive working relationship, complications inevitably arose. The society had no direct authority over the garden's director/manager and had to negotiate differences of opinion through the parks department. Nor could the society decide how or whether to adjust garden operations. In 1990 the botanical garden had already lost a third of its staff due to attrition when further city budget deficit issues mandated citywide staff reductions. The city unilaterally terminated two more workers, a horticulturist and a gardener. When it rained in 1994 the electricity in the conservatory went off, and there was trouble scheduling city repair workers to fix it; the city finally resolved the problem the next year using funds from a federal grant. Staff capacity became an issue again in 2014, when the parks department was forced to cut 10 percent of its budget. That required cuts to parks department workers assigned to the garden even though the garden was running at an appropriate staff level.[213]

It seemed that whenever the city wasn't cutting staff it was pulling workers away to address plant issues elsewhere. Since the garden's director was charged with directing the staff, this in turn distracted the director's attention from the garden. A prime example was the city's new Friedrich Wilderness Park, 232 acres in northwestern Bexar County and a nesting area of the endangered golden-cheeked warbler and black-capped vireo. The city assigned oversight of this park to the botanical garden. In 1988 garden staff began a long-term census of Friedrich's flora and fauna, aided by Trinity University students. In 1995 a Texas Parks and Wildlife grant enabled the parks department to increase Friedrich's own staff from one to four. The next year Friedrich ceased being a drain on the botanical garden when it was transferred to the parks department's horticultural services manager as an independent unit.[214]

A less visible but perhaps even greater challenge was the city's mandated salary level for the garden director, significantly lower than the salary for directors of other gardens. That led to difficulty in finding willing applicants. The resulting delays in hiring caused the garden to be run without a designated director for more than a third of its first twenty-six years.[215]

Furthermore, there was a structural disconnect with the position. The parks department allowed the botanical society to take the lead in interviewing and selecting director candidates. The society wanted candidates with expertise in managing botanical gardens and considered that person to be the director of the garden. The city's agreement with the society, however, put its Parks and Recreation Department director in charge of the garden. The director selected by the society to operate the garden was classified as a lower manager, with a commensurately lower pay grade. Despite the society's repeated offers to make the position more attractive with contributions to raise the pay level, the city rebuffed those offers on the grounds that they violated municipal procedures.

The issue arose with the hiring of the garden's first director, Eric Tschanz, who came in 1982, nearly a year after the city created his position. He departed six years later to become president and executive director of the 807-acre Powell Gardens in suburban Kansas City, Missouri, a position he held for the next twenty-eight years.

Botanical garden veteran Paul Cox, whose usual title was supervisor, served as interim director for nearly two years, until September 1990, when the director's position was filled by Eric Lautzenheiser. Lautzenheiser, who had a degree in horticulture from Texas A&M University and attended the Royal Academy of Landscape Architecture of Sweden, had previously been

Garden directors succeeding Eric Tschanz included (*from left*) Eric Lautzenheiser, Dave Stockdale, and Bob Brackman.

assistant director of the Armand Bayou Nature Center, director of the Mercer Arboretum near Houston, and a nursery and landscaping business operator. Most recently he had been a parks department staff member already assigned to the botanical garden but tasked with managing the city's Friederich Wilderness Park. In 1997 he resigned to become superintendent of the San Antonio Parks and Recreation Department Nature Preserves. Cox again assumed the mantle of interim director.

The cycle soon repeated itself. Dave Stockdale, a Purdue University graduate in agriculture who had been director of education at the University of Washington Center for Urban Horticulture and Washington Park Arboretum in Seattle, was named director in January 1999. Four years later he left to become project manager for the new Hughson Arboretum and Gardens in central California. Cox again took over as interim director, aided by the society's new managing director, Candace Andrews.

By this time society leaders had tired of the directorship merry-go-round and the logistical difficulties with the city in shaping policies of the entity the society was committed to support. "It was doable but not easy," recalled Susan Lane, board president at the millennium, as the society began to face the inevitability of having to begin a new era. "We just couldn't keep operating that way."[216]

Lane's successor in 2001, Claire Alexander, and the executive committee all saw the solution in the San Antonio Zoological Society's handling of a similar issue more than a half century

Botanical society presidents who followed each other in office included (*from left*) Nancy Zachry, Susan Lane, and Claire Alexander.

before, when the privately run zoological society took over the parks department's operational control of the San Antonio Zoo, relieving the city of the expense of running the zoo during the Depression.

The city had already, in 1997, informally approached the botanical society with the same proposal. It would permit the society to manage the garden independently while still, like the zoo, receiving an annual city subsidy. But the society had demurred, daunted by its need to generate far greater revenue and to create a large endowment to run the garden itself, even with the city subsidy. Now, with another difficult director search under way and a static city budget with no allowance even for inflation, the society realized that it needed to face up to the challenges and think creatively.[217]

In 2004 Alexander offered a quid pro quo to new parks and recreation director Malcolm Matthews: if he would accept a subsidy to increase the salary for a new director qualified to oversee the change to private management, the botanical society would agree to the transition and begin planning for it.[218]

The city agreed. It amended the original 1981 operating agreement to increase the director's annual salary with $20,000 donated by the society; the position would still be classified at the manager level and remain wholly under city control. The agreement would automatically renew upon the city's receipt of each year's contribution of the salary supplement. To fulfill its part of the bargain, the society reestablished a long-range planning committee to develop plans to increase the society's annual revenues by at least $1 million and to take over full operational management of the garden from the city.[219]

The society's founding patron, Gilbert Denman Jr., had died in 2004 at eighty-three, before the transition began. But his grants administrator at the Ewing Halsell Foundation, Robert Washington, had been a strong supporter of the society from the start and was a founding director. Foundation trustees signaled their enthusiasm for the society to assume independent management with a $1 million challenge grant to start an endowment fund for the Lucile Halsell Conservatory, the garden's biggest maintenance expense. The grant required the society to raise an additional $100,000 for the conservatory endowment each year for five years, ultimately adding $1.5 million, today's equivalent of $2.5 million.[220]

The salary subsidy worked as intended. The fourth director, Bob Brackman, was found and hired with little further delay. Brackman, who held a degree in ornamental horticulture and landscape design from the University of Tennessee, came in January 2006 from Nashville, where he had been director for thirteen years of the Cheekwood Botanical Garden and Arboretum and, before that, director of horticulture at the new Dallas Arboretum and Botanical Garden. His twelve-year tenure in San Antonio encompassed crucial transitions and helped set the garden on the path to strong organization and management.

Dinosaurus Tex in 2002 was the first show to attract large crowds. Dinosaur enthusiast George Blasing entranced one group of young visitors.

Steve Tobin produced more than twenty root sculptures exhibited in the garden in 2022.

A Lively Place

With its roots established, the San Antonio Botanical Garden could focus more attention on programs to reach traditional audiences and underserved communities. They responded. Annual attendance that was counted in the hundreds in the opening year of 1980 rose to 17,000 in 1991 and 28,000 by 2008. The garden's geographical draw broadened. The latest surveys showed that a third of visitors were from San Antonio, a third from elsewhere in Texas, and the rest from outside the state. Growing awareness translated into community support as the botanical society's paid membership climbed from 1,600 in 1997 to more than 2,700 in 2008.[221]

Headline events drew record crowds and became significant profit centers. The first such major event was the three-month *Dinosaurus Tex* spectacle in 2002, inspired by a visit made by society president Nancy Zachry and board member Cathy Garison to Ste. Genevieve, Missouri, to view dinosaur models by paleontologist Guy Darrough. The resulting show of three-dimensional figures of prehistoric animals throughout the garden was a turning point, the garden's first event to draw major corporate sponsors—H-E-B and SBC Communications, later AT&T—and to attract large crowds. A repeat of the show three years later helped turn a month's predicted loss of $44,500 into a $22,500 profit.

As Bob Brackman settled into his post as the garden's fourth director, in 2007 the botanical society partnered with Nickelodeon to host the nation's first exhibit of *Dora and Diego's Garden Adventure* in a botanical or nature garden setting. Large models of cartoon characters Dora the Explorer and Diego introduced young children to the plant world. Opening day drew 11,000 visitors. The run drew many visitors who might not have otherwise come to the garden and yielded a desired by-product, more than 500 new members for the society. In 2014 *Nature Connects—Art with Lego Bricks* set a new attendance record of 35,781.

When construction projects took onsite parking spots in 2015, the society reached an agreement with AT&T down the hill at the intersection of Hildebrand

Artificial lighting supplemented moonlight at an amphitheater concert during Gardens by Moonlight, which also offered an array of snacks and a closeup view of the moon.

Avenue and Broadway to provide remote parking spaces as well as shuttle buses to garden events.

Wide-ranging functions numbered more than two hundred each year, including tours and summer camps plus the ever-popular Children's Vegetable Garden and Little Sprouts, a garden activity program for preschool children. There were Brews and Blooms in September, Wine Down at the Garden in October, BOOtanica at Halloween, and Family Flashlight Night in November. Viva Botanica, a weekend of events first held in spring 1983, was an early staple of garden entertainment but had faded in popularity by 2006. It was replaced with Walk Across Texas, only to be revived five years later.

The botanical society launched Art in the Garden in 2004 with works by Danville Chadbourne and the next year featured the *trabajo rústico* of Carlos Cortés. Gardens by Moonlight offered nighttime glimpses of the full moon from the garden's winding trails. Until private funding provided electric trailside

A twenty-five-foot-high dragon in an Art in the Garden exhibition from Montreal was made up of 14,916 plants needing daily watering and weekly trimming. Among other shows were metal origami sculptures by Kevin Box and mosaic bunnies by Hunt Slonem.

A Lego exhibition in 2014 set an attendance record for garden-wide exhibitions.

A hound named Baskerville surveys the garden during Dog Days in 2023.

Katie Erickson, the garden's vice president of learning and interpretation, displays a planting plan for the WaterSaver Community, mini house facades surrounded by low-water landscapes (*facing page*).

lighting, volunteers and staff prepared and placed "hundreds of kerosene lanterns" along the trails, then picked them up and cleaned and stored them for the next year.[222]

In 2023 the garden hosted a spectacle that combined art and horticulture. Produced by Mosaïcultures Internationales de Montréal, *Imaginary Worlds* featured eight plant-covered sculptures throughout the garden. All were constructed around steel frames covered with layers of steel mesh, sphagnum moss, and potting mix wrapped in black cloth, with plant roots reaching through holes punched in the fabric.

Designers selected plants for the surfaces based on appropriate colors, textures, shapes, and tolerance to the South Texas summer heat. A peacock in one garden took 1,344 plants, and a mermaid at the East Texas lake took 3,122. Largest by far was a twenty-five-foot-high dragon in the Lucile Halsell Conservatory using 14,916 plants and taking 468.5 hours to complete. The dragon guarded black pots filled with golden barrel cacti resembling pots of gold. At its feet, celosias, coleus, and Powis Castle artemisia resembled fire and smoke. Staff hand-watered the sculptures daily and pruned them weekly with sheep shears to maintain the shapes of the skin and faces.[223]

Architects in 2008 displayed nine artistic interpretations of treehouses, cosponsored by the local chapter of the American Institute of Architects. It was the first of several architecture-based exhibits. Chocolate Day drew 1,200 visitors in 2011. Dog Days drew 240 dogs and 920 people in 2012, despite the unexpected September heat.

Some programs concentrated more heavily on horticultural education and water conservation, a key focus of the garden in recent decades. Xeriscape, a self-sustaining demonstration garden at the western edge of the botanical garden, evolved in 2004 into WaterSaver Lane nearby. Finished in collaboration with the San Antonio Water System, it featured a row of six small house fronts with varying styles of lawns and landscaping. More than a hundred identified plant species illustrated the versatility of low-water-use landscapes that work in South Texas.

In 2023 the garden transformed WaterSaver Lane into WaterSaver Community, designed by MP Studio with input from garden board member and landscape architect Elaine

WATERSAVER COMMUNITY

Sales volunteer Lan Eng plucks dry stems from a flat carried by Wally McGee.

Longtime chair of plant sales was Beth Wrockloff, seated at far left beside Al Guzman and Ruth Rea, who helped revive the sales program in the late 1990s.

Kearney and support from the San Antonio Water System and San Antonio River Authority. Facades of eco-friendly construction and a variety of landscapes showcase dry shade gardens, water management techniques, and plantings according to sun exposure and soil conditions. The separate Kyse WaterSaver Garden, near the conservatory, was redesigned and replanted under Tres Fromme in 2021.[224]

The garden improved its own water conservation efforts in 2021 by expanding its four years of use of city-supplied recycled water and converting water in the East Texas lake to recycled water, reducing the garden's fresh-water consumption by more than two-thirds.

In 2018 more than three hundred people attended the Incredible Edible Insect Event, a food and plant conservation program with an entomology talk, chef demonstrations, and a four-course tasting of edible bugs. Fire ants spiced a sweet potato mousse, and fire ant queso was served with Chirp Chips—tortilla chips made with cricket flour. An instructor with the sponsor, Texas A&M AgriLife Extension Service in Bexar County, noted that eating insects "is not only practical and sustainable; it can also be very tasty."[225]

Volunteers stepped up as workers and docent tour leaders to provide extra help for garden staff, still employed by the Parks and Recreation Department. In 2009 more than two hundred volunteers assisted with Fourth Friday Plant Walks and Saturday Bird Walks. During summer droughts they pruned and planted and watered. When the 2010–11 winter brought sixty-five hours of sustained subfreezing temperatures, volunteers saved staff workers "hundreds of hours" by cutting back freeze damage and replanting. Volunteers also formed the backbone of the garden's lucrative plant sales, which totaled $145,000 in 2022. These had been headed since the late 1990s by volunteer Beth Wrockloff and recently by her successor, horticulturist and botanist Mary Irish, the author of several books on southwestern plants and gardening.[226]

Wear and tear led to high-ticket maintenance for such aging features as the carriage house cupola ($25,000 in 2011) and for Kumamoto En ($100,000 in 2004), one of the periodic restorations anticipated when the garden was completed in 1989. In a major repair cycle in 2023–24, Japanese construction workers assembled the new *azumaya*—the tea waiting arbor—that had been precut in Japan. Japanese landscape business owners helped install identical replacements of Kumamoto En's four traditional types of fences with assistance from botanical garden workers headed by Sam Hogg, vice president of operations.

In the Hill Country area, the 1850s barn, one of four log structures in the pioneer farmstead moved to the banks of the East Texas lake, partially collapsed in mid-2017. The garden's buildings and grounds committee had it propped up pending further deliberation. But the log barn was deemed too expensive to restore and was removed in August 2020, and its remains given to a construction worker.[227]

Maintaining the Lucile Halsell Conservatory presented the greatest challenges physically and financially. By 2004 its mechanical systems were in "dire need" of repairs and improvements, to the tune of at least $180,000. Although the botanical society was responsible for the conservatory's upkeep, given its importance to San Antonio, the city reimbursed the society for two-thirds of the cost. But then came more problems—trouble with the temperature in the fern room, issues with settling soil, and the need to replace one hundred panes of glass, most broken by vandals along the still open Funston Place. One person suggested economizing on pest control by letting quail loose inside the conservatory to eat the invaders; that proposal went no further. In 2005 the city contributed $500,000 for repairs and the Ewing Halsell Foundation added $100,000 on behalf of the society.[228]

The volume of the conservatory's broken glass dropped precipitously when the society finally purchased the last targeted housing unit remaining on Funston Place in 2008, two decades after purchasing the first. The city contributed $100,000 to demolish those structures still standing. After the Mahncke Park Neighborhood Association withdrew its objection to closing the street, society president Joel Erben could announce in April 2009 that the city had approved the long-sought goal.

A year later, a luncheon in the Palm House capped a three-year general renovation of the conservatory. Honored were two major donors—former board presidents and sisters-in-law Mary Pat Stumberg and Nancy Zachry—plus representatives of the Ewing Halsell and Elizabeth Huth Coates foundations. Those attending applauded installation of the final pane of new glass, complete with a huge pink bow.[229]

WELCOME TO THE GARDEN

Closing Funston Place allowed the garden to add eight acres and a new entrance.

Independent at Last

Two long-awaited events within sixteen months of each other in 2009 and 2010 enabled fundamental changes to the garden's development and operations. Purchase of the last house on Funston Place across from the garden finally triggered closing of that section of the street, allowing the San Antonio Botanical Society to resume its long-delayed planning for eight acres along the garden's southern border. Then the framework for the garden's operational independence from the city was put together.

In October 2010 the society and the city finalized an agreement to begin the first phase of its garden operations independent of the city. For a trial period of nine years the city would no longer oversee the garden but would lease it to the society. Garden director Bob Brackman would be employed not by the Parks and Recreation Department but by the society. The society no longer needed a managing director, so Candace Andrews became the garden's director of community relations and visitor services. Garden workers remained employed and paid by the city but were under Brackman's management.[230]

During this time the city would still fund the cost of operations. One city official suggested the society would need less money, since the society might be able to run things more efficiently than the city could. The trial period would provide time to test new procedures, process transfers of inventory and contractual obligations from city to society, and allow employees to decide whether they wanted to stay at the garden or remain employed by the city elsewhere. The final changeover was set for January 1, 2019.[231]

The deadline required the botanical society to be able to run the garden smoothly and to substantially increase its revenue stream to support operations. A key to that success would be figuring out how to utilize the newly added Funston tract. The society commissioned a wide-ranging strategic plan by the Saint Louis–based firm EMD Consulting. After the strategic plan was completed in 2009, the

A 2015 aerial view shows the eight acres added to the southern edge of the garden between the vertical dirt path of the former Funston Place, right of center, and Pinckney Street at left. North New Braunfels Avenue is the horizontal street across the top.

society retained MESA Design Group of Dallas to draw up a site plan.[232]

MESA Design Group submitted an eighty-two-page master site plan in August 2010. It would dramatically enhance the garden with an entrance area partway up the former Funston Place, with new gardens and attractions beyond. An event center complex near the carriage house would face a redesigned lawn. The total cost was $40 million.

There was enough time to prepare a proposal to include the Funston tract development in the May 2012 city bond package, leaving the event center for later. Voters approved $1.2 million for the garden. Texas Parks and Wildlife gave another $1 million. That gave the society confidence to hire Weddle Gilmore Architects of Scottsdale, Arizona, known for blending their projects with their surroundings, and Ten Eyck Landscape Architects of Austin.

While Philip Weddle was his firm's chief architect for the project, in an unusual move for the time, a landscape architect—Christine Ten Eyck—was chosen as lead architect. Pape-Dawson civil engineers and Kopplow Construction were selected as the builders. Society board president Karen Greenwood and her husband, board member

A dramatic open entrance replaced the garden's enclosed main entry through the carriage house. The entrance leads along the former Funston Place to, on the south side, the Welcome Building and the Discovery Center, with a passageway between the two buildings into a culinary garden whose bounties have included pequin peppers.

Jim Greenwood, took charge of the capital campaign. In June 2015, when initial fundraising showed that the effort was viable, formal groundbreaking took place for the project, which divided the Funston Place property roughly into thirds.

The westernmost third, closest to North New Braunfels Avenue, was landscaped for parking that would be accessed off a lower section of the former street.

The second third began at the end of the parking area with an entrance plaza and an admissions kiosk that replaced the carriage house as the garden's main entrance. The tiered limestone blocks of the Mays Family Display Garden lay ahead. Two paths led into the main garden, past a new gift shop building to the left. To the right, an entrance through the Halsell Welcome Building and H-E-B Discovery Center opened onto a courtyard. It featured three dozen limestone-bordered beds making up the Zachry Foundation Culinary Garden, where ingredients would be grown for the teaching kitchen of the Goldsbury Foundation Pavilion at the courtyard's far side. Runoff drained into a 29,000-gallon cistern, a significant if invisible water conservation element below. The entry complex and the culinary garden courtyard area opened in October 2017.

The upper third of the new tract became the Family Adventure Garden, a project chaired by board member and landscape architect Marline Lawson. Filled with native Texas plants and fenced to keep children from wandering far, it offered creek beds and groves to play in and a peak to climb. It opened in February 2018.[233]

A Family Adventure Garden with native plants includes faux limestone play areas and a shaded walkway along No Name Creek, near Dry Rock Creek.

Efforts chaired by society president Jeffrey Rochelle then shifted to the garden's western border. The 1980 entry building, by that time converted to offices and a library, was demolished to make way for The Betty Kelso Center, completed in 2019, a LEED Gold-certified venue with 3,500 square feet of event space. Wooden slats on the walls and an upward-sweeping ceiling extending outdoors were cut from logs of sinker cypress recovered from the swamps of East Texas and Louisiana, where they had sunk more than a century before while being transported to sawmills. Grains of these logs, often centuries old when felled, are denser and tighter than those of logs from newer growth trees, providing strong acoustic absorption. Prolonged submersion in water also makes the cypress, which does not rot, exceptionally durable.

The Kelso Center's folding glass doors opened onto a patio fronting the expansive Greehey Lawn. The long, low fountain that previously divided the lawn was gone, unifying the space for audiences seated on the grass when the center's patio served as a stage. The fountain's original water source at the eastern edge of the lawn was preserved in the John L. Santikos Fountain of the Ferns. To the left rose the iconic 1980 wisteria arbor, rehabilitated by the Circle Bar Foundation.

The Betty Kelso Center, completed in 2019, provides a venue for indoor events and opens onto a patio that can also serve as a stage for viewers on the lawn beyond.

Sabina Carr (*left*) became director in 2019 and was succeeded as president and CEO four years later by Katherine Trumble (*right*).

An administration building went up past the northern end of the Sullivan Carriage House.

Completion of the entire project brought the garden acclaim of the type not received since the conservatory opened thirty years before. The American Institute of Architects presented the botanical garden with its prestigious Architecture Award. *Architectural Digest* listed the San Antonio Botanical Garden, along with the Atlanta Botanical Garden and California's Huntington Botanical Gardens, as one of "the eight most beautifully designed botanical gardens in America."[234]

By the end of 2019, both four years of continuous construction and the trial operations period with the city had been successfully wrapped up. As the botanical society formally took charge of the garden from the city, a new director, Sabina Carr, arrived. Carr, who came from Atlanta in November following the resignation of Bob Brackman, had been vice president of marketing for the Atlanta Botanical Garden for seventeen years after working in media and marketing. She had also served a term as president of the American Public Gardens Association.[235]

Carr was confronted with the COVID-19 pandemic early in 2020, which caused the gardens to close in March. Staff maintained the Children's Vegetable Garden and the culinary garden, which contributed more than a thousand pounds of food to those suffering from the pandemic. The outdoor campus offered plenty of room for the social distancing sought during the pandemic, and garden operations resumed two months later. During this time the society managed to raise 80 percent of its annual budget, and the annual fund exceeded its goal. With the help of nearly $1 million from the Small

Figures in bright colors favored by painter Frida Kahlo were part of the 2021 *Frida Kahlo Oasis* exhibition.

A traditional garden featuring celosia marigolds, pentas, and cannas is among those getting seasonal replanting, and the occasional tour led by Andrew Labay (*below*), the garden's chief mission officer.

Business Administration's Paycheck Protection Program, operations were back on track toward board president Omar Akhil's goal of the institution becoming "a world-class garden."[236]

Pre-pandemic attendance levels returned after May 2021, when the *Frida Kahlo Oasis* opened. The exhibit featured a stylized representation of the noted painter's home and gardens in Mexico City, monumental animals that often appeared in her artworks, and attenuated oversize figures clad in the bright colors and designs of Kahlo's own clothing. The six-month show drew 126,000 visitors.

Lightscape opened in 2021 with fifteen displays along a one-mile path. Its control center was in the Auld House, its blue interior lighting making occupancy unnoticed by nighttime passersby.

Total attendance that year reached 367,000, and by 2025 it was exceeding 400,000. Memberships surpassed 12,000. Under Katie Erickson, vice president of learning and interpretation, attendance on school tours rose to 31,000 a year, with 60 percent from schools in low-income neighborhoods.

The holiday season's *Lightscape*, fifteen monumental light displays along a one-mile path, began a three-year run in 2021. It included a field of dancing bluebonnets and a cathedral tunnel with a hundred thousand lights. The season's thirty-three-day spectacular in 2024 and 2025 was *Illuminate*, featuring handcrafted lanterns and botanically focused larger-than-life silken sculptures lighted from within.

The change of exhibition happened to coincide with the departure of Sabina Carr, who became president and CEO of the Dallas Arboretum and Botanical Garden, and the appointment in November 2023 of Katherine Trumble, director of development at the San Antonio Botanical Garden since 2020, as interim director. Six months later Trumble was named president and CEO. When a narrow wedge of nearly one acre along Old Austin Road below the garden's southeastern

Illuminate, the winter light spectacle beginning in 2024, featured bright vistas of interior-lit silken flowers, plants, insects, and animals.

corner became available, she saw a new opportunity. Though awkwardly located for visitor use, it was an ideal spot for maintenance facilities that took up prime space in the garden.

The garden's reaction to Trumble's proposal was a measure of its newfound capability to maneuver independently and decisively. There was no time to wait for a purchase price to be appropriated in a future city bond issue, and getting immediate funding elsewhere seemed unlikely. Trumble, with board chair Phil Miller, began negotiations. The botanical society dipped into its own reserves and bought the property in 2024, adding its first piece of directly owned land to the rest of the property, owned by the city.[237]

The tract added an unlikely dimension to the history of the garden's site. It had been vacant until World War I, when Fort Sam Houston rapidly expanded and the sprawling Camp Travis was built east of Old Austin Road. Travis Mercantile Company soon opened a store on the civilian side of Old Austin Road, at the southwest corner with Pinckney Street. A succession of tenants in a newer building followed, among them a beauty shop, liquor store, and dress shop.

The site's longest tenant was the Old Time Wooden Nickel Company, established in 1948 by the noted San Antonio magic shop owner and magician Louis Berkowitz. In his first year Berkowitz produced ten thousand wooden nickels and stamped them by hand. In 1995 his successor moved the company to Old Austin Road and increased production. Tourists were attracted to its adjoining museum, which displayed old equipment and more than one million wooden nickels. A few years after closing the museum the company's owners faced sharply increasing property taxes, causing them to sell their property and move the business to Clearwater, Florida.[238]

Trumble was also focusing on a master plan undertaken by the Massachusetts-based planning group Reed Hilderbrand, a ten- to fifteen-year reimagining of the garden. Trumble said the plan, coming "at an inflection point in the garden's history," would include further development of plant conservation and improved accessibility. A concurrent initiative would be the Texas Recovery for Ecological and Environmental Stability, or TREES, conceived by the garden's Andrew Labay and Michael Eason, which would reforest the banks along the Guadalupe River in nearby Kerr County with fifty thousand native trees to restore habitat devastated by Hill Country flooding in 2025. Months later the Community Foundation for the Texas Hill Country awarded the project a $2 million grant and a separate $1 million matching grant.

A projected $100 million capital campaign, Garden Dreams: The San Antonio Botanical Garden Campaign for Plants, People and Lives, was established to fund the master

Toasting the garden's forty-fifth anniversary at the 2025 gala were (*from left*) Julie Wilkinson, board chair; Bill Scanlan, event chair and former board member; and Katherine Trumble, garden president and CEO.

Sam Hogg (*second from right*), vice president of operations, stands next to consultant Howard Kinsel as two technicians test sealant applications on replacement glass panels to be lifted onto the Lucile Halsell Conservatory.

plan. Chaired by Dacia and Lanham Napier, the campaign was announced at the same time 2025 was designated a year of celebration for the garden's forty-fifth anniversary.

An early improvement relating to the master plan began in 2024—a two-year, $8.3 million refurbishing of the Lucile Halsell Conservatory. It included updating environmental controls, lighting improvements, and new hardware for opening and closing vents. Most noticeably, the conservatory's 1,200 panes of glass, clouded over time, were replaced with new panes, spreading a renewed sparkle along the conservatory's far-flung sight lines across the garden.[239]

Also new was the Napier Orchid Pavilion, transforming the circular exhibit room near the conservatory entrance as a cloud forest displaying the garden's orchid collection and expanding it from 150 to 600 species. The orchids are slated to become the first accredited orchid collection in Texas.

The garden's traditional maintenance and greenhouse area, which had been mostly off limits to visitors, would be open to the public. Aided by the impending move of maintenance facilities, a new conservation and education building would become a center for Southwest botanical research—designed by the New York firm SO–IL—with classrooms and research space and a regional seed bank, herbarium, and small library.

The Hill Country area near the Schumacher house would reflect viticulture in Texas with planting of a one-acre display vineyard. That happened to fit the background of Andrew Labay, the garden's chief mission officer and previously a viticulture program specialist with Texas A&M AgriLife Extension. The vineyard would grow a range of grapes, including Texas natives, to be used in the garden's culinary education program.

A reimagining of the garden ten to fifteen years in the future includes turning the conservatory's circular exhibit room into the Napier Orchid Pavilion.

In a coincidence of history, the planned vineyard's location was on land once owned by François Guilbeau Jr., who had sold the adjacent site for the reservoir in 1878. It may have nurtured some of the hardy grapevines that grew on Guilbeau's San Antonio properties. In 1876–78 Guilbeau shipped several hundred tons of root cuttings from his vines to Europe, where an epidemic of root disease was killing grapevines. His cuttings were among those grafted to replace diseased roots, saving the European wine industry.[240]

Harking back to a more recent heritage was news from the Ewing Halsell Foundation. Through Gilbert Denman Jr. in 1974 it had made the critical donation that launched the botanical garden on its distinctive course, the first of several grants the foundation made at pivotal times. In November 2025 the foundation announced the first major gift, for $5 million, to the Garden Dreams campaign. It was the largest gift from an individual donor in the garden's history, one that likewise seemed destined to foreshadow new levels of achievement by the San Antonio Botanical Garden.

SAN ANTONIO BOTANICAL GARDEN

In 2026 the garden adopted a new logo, designed by the Butler design firm, evoking biodiversity.

South Texas
Old Austin Road
Halsell Way
East Texas Pineywoods and Lake
Texas Native Trail
Lucile Halsell Conservatory
Hill Country
Family Adventure Garden
Entrance
Pinckney Street
Funston Place
N. New Braunfels Ave
Destinations and Amenities
1 Halsell Welcome Building
2 H-E-B Discovery Center
3 The Zachry Foundation Culinary Garden
4 Goldsbury Foundation Pavilion/ CHEF Teaching Kitchen
5 Mays Family Display Garden
6 Kumamoto En Japanese Garden
7 Sensory Garden
8 The Betty Kelso Center
9 Greehey Lawn
10 John L. Santikos Fountain of the Ferns
11 Circle Bar Foundation Wisteria Arbor
12 Sullivan Carriage House/ Restaurant
13 Richmond Plaza
14 Rose and Old-Fashioned Gardens
15 Sacred Garden
16 WaterSaver Community
17 Kyse WaterSaver Garden
18 Overlook and Acequia
19 Amphitheater
20 Cactus and Succulent Garden
21 Children's Vegetable Garden
22 Event Tent
23 Exhibit Room
24 Kleberg Desert Pavilion
25 Northrup Tropical Room
26 Palm and Cycad Pavilion
27 Fern Grotto
28 Texas Native Trail Pavilion
29 Auld House
30 Schumacher House
31 East Texas Log Cabin
32 Bird Watch
33 Adobe House
Key
Restrooms
Food
Gift Shop
Water
Parking

Notes

ABBREVIATIONS USED IN THE NOTES

Express	*San Antonio Express, San Antonio Daily Express, San Antonio Express-News*
Light	*San Antonio Light, San Antonio Daily Light*
Minutes	San Antonio Botanical Society / Garden board of directors and executive committee minutes, San Antonio Botanical Garden
News	*News from the Botanical Garden, News from the San Antonio Botanical Garden*
SABG	San Antonio Botanical Garden archives, San Antonio Botanical Garden
SAPL	San Antonio Public Library, Texana Room
SAWS	San Antonio Water System
Times	*North San Antonio Times*
Vibrante	*Vibrante, the Member Magazine of the San Antonio Botanical Garden*

Introduction

1 Anders Saustrup to Gilbert Denman, Jan. 22, 1980, SABG; Minutes, Dec. 7, 1981.

2 Minutes, Dec. 7, 1981, Apr. 6, 1982; Gilbert M. Denman, "The Development of the San Antonio Botanical Society" (1987), 1, SABG.

3 Emilio Ambasz & Associates, "Et in Arcadia Ambasz," *Architectural Record*, Sept. 1984, 120; Herbert Muschamp, "Herbert Muschamp on Architecture," *New Republic*, Dec. 19, 1988, 26.

4 Maggie Malone, "True Splendor," *Newsweek*, Sept. 12, 1988, 68.

5 City Ordinance 55323, "Authorizing the Construction of a Conservatory," May 13, 1982; William Aldrich, "New Texas Greenhouse," *Chicago Tribune*, Dec. 1, 1985, 21.

6 Minutes, June 4, 1984.

7 As a foundation note expressed about another project, "Will select contractor . . . so as to insure the best professional job possible and to remove this decision from the political process." Undated memo ca. 1978, SABG.

8 Emilio Ambasz to Hall Hammond, Aug. 30, 1983, SAPL; Minutes, June 4, 1984, Sept. 9, 1985; "$6.5 Million Conservatory," *Times*, Aug. 22, 1985, 7; "Conservatory Completion," *News* (Fall 1987); SABG oral history interview with Dan Wigodsky, Nov. 1, 2024, 21–22. Wigodsky was an architect with Jones and Kell. Other major contributions were $300,000 from the Robert J. Kleberg Jr. and Helen C. Kleberg Foundation for the desert pavilion, $250,000 from Gretchen Cook Northrup for the tropical pavilion, and $50,000 from Walter and Lenora Brown.

9 Minutes, Feb. 27, 1989.

10 Minutes, July 31, 1984.

11 Minutes, Sept. 21, Oct. 7, Oct. 21, 1985, Nov. 17, 1986; William Aldrich, "New Texas Greenhouse," *Chicago Tribune*, Dec. 1, 1985, 21; Paul Cox, "In Search of Plants for the Conservatory," *News* (Summer 1986).

12 Minutes, Sept. 9, 1985.

13 Paul Goldberger, "Sunken Garden to Bloom," *New York Times*, June 11, 1987, 17.

14 The desert room's temperature today is kept at 94 degrees in the day and 72 at night, with humidity below 65 percent. Hot tropical conservatory temperatures are 80 to 90 degrees in the day and 70 to 80 at night.

15 "Conservatory Completion," *News* (Fall 1987). Speakers at the session at the St. Anthony Hotel included Emilio Ambasz and three other nationally known architects, Cesar Pelli, Edward Larrabee Barnes, and Alan Taniguchi. Panelists at the Trinity session included directors of the Royal Botanic Gardens at Kew, the Chicago Botanic Garden, and the Honolulu Botanical Gardens, plus a representative of the New York Botanical Garden.

16 Loydean Thomas, "Lucile Halsell Conservatory," *Express*, Feb. 29, 1988, 10-A; Herbert Muschamp, "Herbert Muschamp on Architecture," *New Republic*, Dec. 19, 1988, 26. Three days earlier Mayor Henry Cisneros had signed City Ordinance 66654, formally accepting the botanical society's gift of the conservatory to the city of San Antonio.

17 Paul Goldberger, "Sunken Garden to Bloom," *New York Times*, June 11, 1987, 17.

A Dozen Tries since 1884

18 *Light*: "City Council," Mar. 25, 1884, 1; "Back to Texas," July 18, 1888, 4.

19 "To Be Opened Tomorrow," *Light*, June 24, 1885, 4.

20 Pratik Patil, "9 Oldest Botanical Gardens in the World," Oldest.org, Mar. 18, 2025, www.oldest.org/nature/botanical-gardens, retrieved Mar. 24, 2025.

21 "Brackenridge Suggests," *Express*, Sept. 20, 1911, 16.

22 *Express*: "State Botanical Garden," July 31, 1914, 6; "Favors Botanical Garden," Dec. 29, 1915, 4. Austin's Lady Bird Johnson Wildflower Center eventually gained the designation of the state's official botanical garden and arboretum.

23 *Light*: "Fair in 1918," Jan. 6, 1916, 1; "Bond Issue," Apr. 30, 1916, 3.

24 "City Botanical Garden," *Light*, Jan. 7, 1917, 5; Fisher, *Brackenridge*, 84. The thirty-eight-acre Busch Gardens, begun by Adolphus Busch in 1905, became world famous, with peak attendance of 1.5 million in 1915, but closed during the Depression. Its land was sold for development.

25 *Light*: "Work Started," Jan. 14, 1917, 8; "Lambert Gets Federal Help," Sept. 16, 1917, 1.

26 "Lambert Gets Federal Help," *Light*, Sept. 16, 1917, 1; "Just Among Ourselves," *San Antonio Evening News*, Nov. 6, 1919, 6.

27 "New Plan for Park," *Light*, Jan. 24, 1933, 5-A.

28 *Express*: "Botanical Garden," Mar. 30, 1934, 18; "Mahncke Park Named City Botanical Garden," June 29, 1934, 9; "Think," July 2, 1934, 1; "10 and 20 Years Ago," *Light*, June 28, 1944, 16.

29 *Express*: "Business Women to Plant Gardens," June 30, 1935, 2-A; "Woman's Responsibility," Mar. 15, 1936, 45.

30 "Women Select Garden Chiefs," *Express*, June 21, 1934, 9.

31 Quillin and Woolford, *Witte Memorial Museum*, 307. *Express*: "Garden Club," Mar. 12, 1931, 8; "Among the Clubs," July 3, 1931, 8, Sept. 3, 1931, 8, Nov. 1, 1933, 6; "Alamo Heights," Feb. 3, 1932, 11; "Illustrated Lecture," Feb. 28, 1932, 4-A; "One of Oldest," Nov. 16, 1952, 6-B. *Light*: "San Antonio Chapter," Dec. 10, 1931, 6; "Society," Apr. 15, 1932, 14; "Alamo Heights," Mar. 1, 1933, 4-A; "Breakfast for Five," Jan. 3, 1939, 3-B. Eight clubs known to have been organized by the time of the garden center's formation were Alamo

Heights–Terrell Hills, Harlandale, Lantana, Laurel Heights, Live Oak, Olmos Park–Park Hill–Monte Vista, Wednesday Morning, and Woodlawn Hills. In November 1932 the San Antonio Garden Club, under the leadership of Harriet Witt, held its first flower show, in the Ruiz House at the Witte Museum. The Witte's entrepreneurial cofounder, Ellen Schulz Quillin, enlisted members to help landscape the grounds.

A San Antonio Garden Club had been proposed in March 1912 by the San Antonio Civic League and the Real Estate Exchange with the goal of beautifying the city's vacant lots in the service of real estate. Its existence was apparently as brief as that of a contemporary garden club sponsored by the San Antonio Chamber of Commerce to "keep something growing the year around and in the long run cut down the high cost of living." *Light*: "Garden Club," Mar. 24, 1912, 43; "Sells Onion Sets," Mar. 4, 1918, 5.

32 Quillin and Woolford, *Witte Memorial Museum*, 304, 307–8; "Garden Center," *Express*, Feb. 6, 1940, 8-A. In 1937 Lucretia Murphy organized Christ Episcopal Church's long-running annual Home and Garden Pilgrimage.

33 Quillin and Woolford, *Witte Memorial Museum*, 308. *Express*: "San Antonio's Treasure," Apr. 26, 1942, 10; "Garden Center's Work," Dec. 1, 1949, 8.

34 *Light*: "Charter for Center," Mar. 4, 1955, 27; "P. A. Renton Jr., Botanical Center," Mar. 6, 1960, 2-H. *Express*: "Garden Center," Nov. 8, 1959, 6-F; "Lecture-Demonstration," Sept. 9, 1964, 2-D.

35 *Light*: "Flower Show," Jan. 18, 1955, 16, and Mar. 10, 1955, 43; P. A. Renton Jr., "Show at Coliseum," Mar. 13, 1955, 19-C. *Express-News*: "Garden Center," July 25, 1954, 4-E; "Garden Center," Nov. 8, 1959, 6-F. So that it could own a new building as a legal entity, the San Antonio Garden Center was chartered as a nonprofit organization in March 1955.

36 "Use of Mahncke Park," *Express*, Sept. 21, 1956, 10; "Water Board Retreats," *Light*, Jan. 10, 1958, 8.

37 *Light*: "Refurbishing of Park," Oct. 20, 1952, 5; "S. A. Swim Pools," July 19, 1953, 18-A. There may also have been another stirring for a botanical garden at Brackenridge Park, known only from a map published by the Paul Anderson Company in 1958 that identified the park nursery south of the Witte Museum as "Botanical Garden."

38 "Use of Mahncke Park," *Express*, Sept. 21, 1956, 10. *Light*: "Water Board Retreats," Jan. 10, 1958, 8; "A Rosier View," Nov. 28, 1964, 14.

39 *Express*: "Deed Is Presented," Feb. 4, 1960, 1-B; "Mahncke Park," Nov. 29, 1962, 18. "City to Call," *Light*, Jan. 24, 1963, 26.

40 "Garden Asked," *Express-News*, July 9, 1964, 72; "Council to Meet," *Express*, July 15, 1964, 5-A.

41 *Express*: "$147,000 Complex," Aug. 28, 1964, 46; "City Okays," Oct. 30, 1964, 10-A. *Light*: "A Rosier View," Nov. 28, 1964, 14; "Garden Center," July 23, 1965, 18.

42 "Austin Rd. Extension," *Express*, Feb. 5, 1965, 8-D; "Christmas Tour," *Light*, Nov. 8, 1964, 1-F.

43 *Express*: "City Okays," Oct. 30, 1964, 10-A; "Mahncke Park Plan," July 23, 1965, 12-D; "A Rosier View," *Light*, Nov. 28, 1964, 14. Credit for working out details with the city went to the garden center's building cochairs, Louise Briggs and Irene Turner.

44 *Light*: "Garden Center In," "Garden Center Opens," Oct. 25, 1966, 29–30. *Express*: "Garden Area," Oct. 27, 1966, 1-B; "Garden Center," Mar. 28, 1976, 3-E. Designed by J. Fred Buenz and enlarged by half ten years later with the Adele Frost Horticulture Hall, the garden center included a paneled library, kitchen, an auditorium that could seat 325, and workspaces including a fifteen-foot counter with sink for flower arranging.

45 "Club Backs," "Botanical Garden," *Light*, Oct. 25, 1966, 29.

A Reservoir in Washington Heights

46 *Tenth Census of the United States, 1880: Water Power* (U.S. Census Office, 180), 254; Fisher, *Brackenridge*, 29–31.

47 *Express*: "Water Works Proposition," Apr. 5, 1877, 4; "The Waterworks Reservoir," Mar. 26, 1879, 4; Maria Watson Pfeiffer, "The San Antonio Botanical Gardens," 1, SABG. The familiar but mistaken belief that the reservoir was built on a quarry site originates in Black, *An Historical and Archaeological Assessment* (1976), which relied on the 1877 contract terms that the reservoir was to be located on "the upper part of the rock quarries." Soon after the signing, however, the site was moved to its ultimate location a mile southeast where there were no quarries, only a softer caliche soil base. Austin Road was the main route to Austin until the wider Austin Highway was cut through from Broadway farther north in the 1930s.

48 "Our Waterworks," *Express*, Apr. 8, 1879, 4. Initial reports put reservoir dimensions at 164 square feet, but later maps showed it to be 213 square feet, which, with 6-foot embankments on either side, makes it close enough to 225 feet, the measurement determined by the reliable U.S. Geological Survey in its first topographical map of the area, in 1953. City of San Antonio Water Department Map, 1927; U.S. Geological Survey Map, 1953; Gregg Eckhardt to Lewis F. Fisher, Feb. 22, 2025.

Black's often quoted though flawed *Historical and Archaeological Assessment* in 1976 includes details on the thickness and height of existing reservoir walls but makes no mention of their width and length as specified in contemporary reports, which show that the reservoir was originally square, as do maps through the 1950s—even though photographs of the same years show a rectangular reservoir. Black seems to dodge the issue altogether by also including no measurements in the report's diagram of the rectangular remains. No account could be found of any reconstruction that would explain the discrepancy.

49 *Express*: "Water Works," Aug. 25, 1877, 4; "A Mammoth Puddle," Feb. 18, 1879, 4; "The Waterworks Reservoir," Mar. 26, 1879, 4; "Our Waterworks," Apr. 8, 1879, 4. Fisher, *Brackenridge*, 31.

50 *Express*: "Wanted Immediately," Mar. 5, 1879, 4; "Our Waterworks," Apr. 8, 1879, 4.

51 Fisher, *Brackenridge*, 32.

52 *Express*: "A Mammoth Puddle," Feb. 18, 1879, 4; "Our Hydrant Water," July 7, 1881, 4. A section then remaining of what was termed a "stone aqueduct" was described in Black, *Historical and Archaeological Assessment*, as running from the southwest corner area of the reservoir property east-northeast toward the main reservoir. No other mention or documentation of an aqueduct can be found. Since it barely protruded above the ground and its walls were twenty feet apart, an enormous width for a short aqueduct, this was more likely a surface stormwater drainage channel or an overflow channel from the main

reservoir to the 1887 backup reservoir. Black, *Historical and Archaeological Assessment*, 3; Maria Watson Pfeiffer, "The San Antonio Botanical Gardens," 12, SABG; Eckhardt to Fisher, Feb. 22, 23, 2025.

53 "Our Hydrant Water," *Express*, July 7, 1881, 4.

54 *Light*: "An Ordinance," Jan. 6, 1885, 4; "Pure Water," July 12, 1899, 4; "A Serious Subject," Nov. 29, 1899, 4; "A Mass Meeting," Feb. 14, 1900. City of San Antonio Water Department Map, 1927, SAWS.

55 "Around the Plaza," *Light*, July 17, 1962, 17. It was also tricky to regulate the pumps to keep the reservoir close to full but not overflowing. When supply exceeded demand, overflow spilled onto Austin Road and caused a muddy morass, angering wagon drivers. The fix was to bury an eight-inch pipe from the reservoir beneath Austin Road and carry the overflow to a ditch across Brackenridge's pastures, now part of Fort Sam Houston, to empty a mile east into Salado Creek. Brackenridge critics then falsely accused him of digging the ditch simply to irrigate his pastures with free water. "City News," *Express*, May 23, 1886, 5; "A Few Pointers," *Light*, July 12, 1887, 4.

56 Fisher, *Brackenridge*, 33; Maria Watson Pfeiffer, "The San Antonio Botanical Gardens," 2, SABG; Eckhardt to Fisher, Mar. 11, 2025.

57 McLean, *Romance of San Antonio's Water Supply*, 9; Fisher: *American Venice*, 20; *Brackenridge*, 68. Although the Crystal Ice Company is often credited with the first artesian well into the Edwards, those sources cite a date mistranscribed from Bert McLean's definitive *The Romance of San Antonio's Water Supply and Distribution*, which in reality credits Brackenridge's company with being the first. Credit to Brackenridge is backed up in Robert J. Harding to Terrell Bartlett, Dec. 26, 1924, SAWS files. Eckhardt to Fisher, Feb. 7, 2025.

58 "City's Water Consumption," *Express*, Oct. 22, 1922, 16A.

59 "Water Company Preparing," *Light*, Sept. 16, 1892.

60 Fisher, *Brackenridge*, 68–69.

61 "Chamberlain Invest. Co.," *Light*, Dec. 22, 1892, 30; "Failure of a Big Concern," *New York Times*, July 11, 1893, 3.

62 *Light*: "Mr. Patterson's Return," Aug. 5, 1890, 1; "Chamberlain Invest Co.," Dec. 22, 1892, 30. "Failure of a Big Concern," *New York Times*, July 11, 1893, 3; Cathe Krause, ed., *Alamo Heights, Texas* (Alamo Heights Golden Anniversary Celebration Inc., 1972), 1–2, 6–7; "Streetcars in San Antonio," Texas Transportation Museum, www.txtransportationmuseum.org/history-streetcars, retrieved Feb. 21, 2025. The Alamo Heights Land and Improvement Company was headed by W. J. Ballantyne Patterson, whose surname is preserved in the Alamo Heights artery Patterson Avenue.

63 *Light*: "City Local News," July 16, 1890, 5; "Mr. Patterson's Return," Aug. 5, 1890, 1; "Chamberlain Invest. Co.," Dec. 22, 1892, 30; "Real Estate Transfers," Jan. 4, 1893, 4, and Feb. 1, 1893, 8. Bexar County Plat Book 105, Bexar County Clerk's Office, 18–19. Nor did much work begin on Chamberlain's third San Antonio property, a thousand acres east of Roosevelt Park south of downtown. The appealing "Heights" designation wouldn't pass muster in that mostly level area, but the company tried implying at least some elevation by using the name Park Terrace, "on the uplands east of the Fair grounds, where they catch the pure breezes of the Mexican Gulf fresh from the intervening plains." Elsewhere in Texas, Chamberlain had interests in Corpus Christi and Aransas Pass and in developing Fort Worth's Arlington Heights and Park Place.

64 *Light*: "Real Estate," Aug. 2, 1892, 8; "Building Permits," Apr. 12, 1893, 4. "The Old Schuetzen Verein," *Express*, Oct. 12, 1975, 8. The club moved to Washington Heights from Powder House Hill east of downtown, where city cemeteries were expanding. One member was Adolph Toepperwein, who became a nationally known exhibition marksman.

65 *Light*: "Investors, Attention," June 1, 1892, 1; "Light Flashes," May 9, 1898, 4. "Failure of a Big Concern," *New York Times*, July 11, 1893, 5. In 1909 architect Atlee B. Ayres designed Brackenridge an elaborate home in the northeast corner of Washington Heights, razed after World War II for the Bel Meade subdivision on the estate.

The Curious Case of Mahncke Park

66 Fisher, *Brackenridge Park*, 56, 93.

67 "Parks and Boulevards," *Light*, June 23, 1905, 4; "Boulevard May Be Given," *Express*, June 30, 1905.

68 "Boulevard May Be Given," *Express*, June 30, 1905.

69 "City Accepts New Park," *San Antonio Gazette*, May 9, 1905, 8; J. P. Newcomb, "Memorandum with Reference to Mahncke Park," 1956, SAWS. The *Light*, on May 9, 1905, records a letter from Brackenridge stating that he was donating twenty-five acres that did not include the "reservoir pasture," six fenced acres around the reservoir itself. "Reservoir Property Accepted," *Light*, May 9, 1905, 5. But the deed made ten days later includes title to the reservoir as well and withholds only improvements and water rights, as he did with Brackenridge Park.

The year before, Brackenridge had donated land for the second park, five and a half miles south of Mahncke Park across from Harris Elementary School, now Pershing Elementary. It was eventually named Pershing Park.

70 *Light*: "Another Liberal Offer," May 20, 1905, 7; "Scenic Driveway," Mar. 26, 1911; "Mahncke Park Driveways," Apr. 2, 1911, 26. "May Be Given," *Express*, June 30, 1905; Johnson, *In the Loop*, 168–69.

71 "Mahncke Park," *Light*, Aug. 4, 1905, 3; San Antonio city engineer's map, 1908, SAWS; City of San Antonio Water Department map, 1927, SAWS; U.S. Geological Survey Well Schedule Report, July 18, 1932, SAWS. To keep the new lake from overflowing, a shaft known as a disposal well extended some three hundred feet down. The top of the well pipe rose one foot above the lake's normal water level so it could drain rising water into permeable rock formations below. Analysis of the pipe as a disposal well is by Gregg Eckardt, longtime environmental scientist and senior resource analyst at the San Antonio Water System. Gregg Eckhardt to Lewis Fisher, Feb. 23, 2025.

72 George Brackenridge Deed to the City of San Antonio, May 19, 1905, Vol. 238, 191, Real Property Records of Bear County. Although Brackenridge enjoyed fine wine and good whiskey, he feared that ordinary citizens could not handle such temptations and needed protection from their weaknesses lest they make the parks disreputable and unattractive to women and children.

73 "City Acreage Tract Sold," *Light*, May 24, 1914, 12-B; Maria Olivia Handy, *History of Fort Sam Houston* (Naylor Company, 1951), 76.

74 "Two San Antonio Parks," Jan. 8, 1911, 20.

75 *Light*: "Civic Committee Offers Plan," July 12, 1913, 7; "Mahncke Park Suggested," July 13, 1913, 17.

76 "Mahncke Park to Be Cleared," *Light*, Mar. 15, 1927, 7-A; "To Better Parks," *Express*, June 24, 1915.

77 San Antonio city engineer's map, 1908; "Calls for Bids," *Light*, Dec. 28, 1915, 3; City of San Antonio Water Department map, 1927. The city agreed to contribute half the width of the sixty-foot rights of way while the developers donated the other half, shaving the lower park's width from 300 feet to 240.

78 "City Paying Debts," *Light*, Jan. 22, 1924, 2.

79 "New Plan for Park," *Light*, Jan. 24, 1933, 5-A.

80 *Express*: "City Offers," Nov. 5, 1940, 1; "Corps May Use," Jan. 5, 1941, 2-A.

81 "Ordinance for Funston," *Light*, Apr. 15, 1942, 4-E; Maria Watson Pfeiffer, "The San Antonio Botanical Gardens," 6, SABG.

82 "Water Office Site," *Light*, Jan. 8, 1958, 8.

83 "Water Office Site," *Light*, Jan. 8, 1958, 8.

84 *Light*: "Water Board Retreats," Jan. 10, 1958, 8; "Keep Off!," Jan. 13, 1958, 8. Instead the City Water Board moved from its crowded Market Street offices to City Hall Annex on Dolorosa Street.

Preparing the Site

85 *Express*: "Monument," July 15, 1906, 16; "Fountain Planned," Jan. 24, 1963, 32; "Mahncke Park," Jan. 24, 1964, 32; "Park Fountain," June 17, 1964, 8-D. *Light*: "Mahncke Bust," Aug. 26, 1908, 5; July 23, 1965, 18. The monument's move to Mahncke Park was sparked by renovation of the surrounding golf course.

86 Black, *Historical and Archaeological Assessment*, 3.

87 Andrew Labay to Lewis Fisher, Aug. 19, 2025.

88 "San Antonio Botanical Center Planning and Development Policy," draft, Mar. 12, 1974, 2, SAPL; "Center Long," *Express*, May 2, 1980, 11-W; "Stewart E. King Biography," Cultural Landscape Foundation, Mar. 5, 2024, www.tclf.org/stewart-e-king-biography, retrieved Apr. 20, 2025.

89 "Center Long," *Express*, May 2, 1980, 11-W; Minutes, Nov. 17, 1981, 2.

90 "Bond Proposal," *Light*, Sept. 6, 1970, 8-H. *Express*: "Center Long," May 2, 1980; Jane Ulbrich, "Money Grows," Jan. 8, 1974, 2-B; May 2, 1980, 11-W. "Report of Parks and Recreation Subcommittee for Capital Improvements on Botanical Garden in Mahncke Park," Aug. 1970, SAPL.

91 Robert S. Dewars, "Carpet Grass," *Express*, Nov. 23, 1969, 5-G; "Mahncke Park," Stewart King Collection, Alexander Architectural Archives, University of Texas Libraries, the University of Texas at Austin. Parking for the arboretum was proposed by making Funston and Parland Places single lanes, one way east on Funston and one way west on Parland. The second lanes would be used for curbside parking on the residential sides.

92 "San Antonio Botanical Center Planning and Development Policy," draft, Mar. 12, 1974, 2, SAPL.

93 A. C. Crouch and Mrs. Jack Gamblin, "The Beautifier," Beautify San Antonio Association mailout, undated, SAPL; untitled request, no addressee, Beautify San Antonio Association, undated, SAPL.

94 "The Beautifier," SAPL.

95 *Express*: "Land Swap," Mar. 7, 1974, 15-A; "Drawings Approved," Apr. 2, 1975, 6-A; "Sanctions Due," Nov. 6, 1974, 4-E.

96 Gilbert Denman Jr., "The Development of the San Antonio Botanical Society" (1987), 1, SABG.

97 John Davidson, "A World of Influence," *Express*, Aug. 27, 2000, 1-H.

98 Black, *Historical and Archaeological Assessment*, 5; Maps, SABG; "Recreational, Park Projects," *Express*, Oct. 6, 1972, 7-A; "Botanical Center," *Light*, July 22, 1976, 14-B.

99 Press release, San Antonio Parks Dept., July 16, 1976, SAPL; "Mule-Drawn Plow," *Express*, July 22, 1976, 4-B; Ronald Darner to R. C. Aldridge Jr., July 27, 1976, SAPL.

100 "San Antonio Botanical," *Light*, May 2, 1980, 11-W.

101 "San Antonio Botanical," *Light*, May 2, 1980, 11-W.

102 *Express*: "Around Town," Oct. 26, 1950, 1-A; "Touch, Smell," June 28, 1976, 4-B; Carolyn Elliott, "Garden of Senses," *Northeast Light*, Feb. 10, 1977, 1; "San Antonio Botanical," *Light*, May 2, 1980, 12-W.

103 "San Antonio Botanical," *Light*, May 2, 1980, 12-W.

104 "San Antonio Botanical," *Light*, May 2, 1980, 12-W; "Go Native," *News* (Winter 2003): 1.

105 Denman, "Development," 1; Ronald Darner to Gilbert Denman, July 24, 1978, and similar payment papers at SABG; Anders Saustrup to Gilbert Denman, Jan. 22, 1980, SABG; John Davidson, "A World of Influence," *Express*, Aug. 27, 2000, 1-H; "Anders Saustrup Obituary," *Austin American-Statesman*, Feb. 20, 2008, www.legacy.com/us/obituaries/statesman/name/anders-saustrup-obituary?id=8727838, retrieved Apr. 30, 2025.

106 Gilbert Denman Jr. to Ronald Darner, Feb. 27, 1978, SABG.

107 Rudy Krisch to Parks and Recreation Department, Nov. 30, 1976, SABG; "San Antonio Botanical," *Light*, May 2, 1980, 12-W; "Go Native," *News* (Winter 2003): 1.

108 Rudy Krisch to Joeris and Clauss Construction Co., Aug. 23, 1978, SABG; "San Antonio Botanical," *Light*, May 2, 1980, 12-W. The final cost of installing the log structures was $45,375, today's equivalent of more than $210,000.

109 Darner to Denman, Mar. 6, 1978, SABG; "Go Native," *News* (Winter 2003): 1, 4.

110 Simpson Landscape Co. to Joeris and Clauss, Dec. 29, 1978, and Jan. 31, 1979, SABG; "Go Native," *News* (Winter 2003): 1, 4.

111 "Go Native," *News* (Winter 2003): 4.

112 "Cox Puts Name," *Times*, Mar. 8, 1990, 1; "Go Native," *News* (Winter 2003): 4.

113 "Cox Puts Name," *Times*, Mar. 8, 1990, 1; "Go Native," *News* (Winter 2003): 4; Andrew Labay to Lewis Fisher, Aug. 19, 2025.

114 Simpson Landscape Co. to Joeris and Clauss, Mar. 31, 1980, SABG; "Go Native," *News* (Winter 2003): 4.

115 "San Antonio Botanical," *Light*, May 2, 1980, 12-W.

116 "San Antonio Botanical," *Light*, May 2, 1980, 12-W.

117 Rudy Krisch to Joeris and Clauss, Jan. 21, 1980, and Apr. 20, 1981; SABG Scott Litchke to Lewis Fisher, Nov. 17, 2025.

118 Scott Litchke to Lewis Fisher, Nov. 17, 2025.

119 Simpson Landscape Co. to Joeris and Clauss, May 25, 1981, SABG; "Go Native," *News* (Winter 2003): 4.

120 James Keeter to Gilbert Denman Jr., July 16, 1979, SABG; Ronald Darner to Helen Stieler Crouch, Dec. 10, 1979, SABG.

121 Ronald Darner to Dan Auld, Jan. 31, 1977; Dan Auld to Gilbert Denman Jr., Feb. 11, 1977; Dan Auld to Helen Campbell, Feb. 18, 1977; Ronald Darner to Gibert Denman Jr., Jan. 20, 1978; Ronald Darner to Robert Washington, Dec. 1, 1982, all SABG.

Launching the San Antonio Botanical Garden

122 "Botanical Garden," *Express*, Apr. 27, 1980, 8-A. Entry fees went into effect the next day, seventy-five cents for adults and fifty cents for children fourteen and under. After the first year, adult admission went up to one dollar. The garden was open from 10 a.m. to 8 p.m. Wednesday through Friday and noon to 8 p.m. on weekends, and closed Monday and Tuesday. "Botanical Garden," *Express*, Apr. 27, 1980, 8-A. San Antonio's was the fifth major botanical garden to open in Texas, preceded by the Fort Worth Botanic Garden (1934), Austin's Zilker Botanic Garden (1964), the Amarillo Botanical Gardens (1968), and Humble's Mercer Arboretum and Botanic Garden (1974).

123 Ronald Darner to Gilbert Denman Jr., Mar. 5, 1980, SAPL; Denman, "Development," 1. Darner wrote Denman: "I have talked to the Garden Center ladies about this subject several times. They are interested in supporting such a group but have no desire of it being an appendage or for that matter having any direct or implied relationship to San Antonio Garden Center Inc."

124 Ronald Darner to Gilbert Denman Jr., Mar. 5, 1980, SAPL. Darner added: "I am sure with your long experience in this case that most of this is old hat to you. We are novices at it and could certainly use your help and guidance."

125 Texas Secretary of State, "Certificate of Incorporation of the San Antonio Botanical Society, Inc., Dec. 31, 1980; "Development of the San Antonio Botanical Society" (1987), 2. Usually known as the botanical society, the official name was later changed to San Antonio Botanical Garden Society.

126 Minutes, Feb. 23, 1981. Denman was instrumental in Hammond's selection as president. Hall Hammond to Lewis Fisher, Apr. 21, 2022. To increase public awareness, by 1983 the board was expanded to fifty-six members.

127 "Ordinance 53676 Authorizing Execution of an Agreement with the San Antonio Botanical Center Society," Apr. 23, 1981, SABG. Minutes, Sept. 22, 1981.

128 "San Antonio Botanical," *Light*, May 2, 1980, 12-W; Minutes, Nov. 17, 1981, Feb. 16, 1982, Nov. 1, 1983; "Concession Agreement By and Between the City and the Society," Dec. 9, 1986, SABG. Twenty-two years later the Schumacher house, suffering decay and a leaking roof, was restored under the guidance of Lewis S. Fisher of Fisher Heck Architects.

129 Minutes, Sept. 22, 1981.

130 Minutes, May 7, Oct. 20, 1981; Eric Tschanz to Ed Baca, Aug. 31, 1981, SAPL; John Jeter, "Botanical Center Takes Tschantz," *Times*, May 20, 1982; "Eric N. Tschanz Receives Prestigious 2017 Honorary Life Member Award," American Public Gardens Association, July 27, 2017, www.publicgardens.org/eric-n-tschanz-receives-prestigious-2017-honorary-life-member-award, retrieved Oct. 3, 2025.

131 Eric Tschanz to Ed Baca, Mar. 24, 1982, SAPL; Eric Tschanz to Tom Keeter, Dec. 16, 1982, SAPL.

132 "Plant Rescuers," *Vibrante*, Sept.–Dec. 2024, 23–25.

133 Carol Burkholder to Fernando Arellano, Oct. 13, 1981, SAPL; *News*, Summer 1991, 2.

134 Minutes, July 9, 1990.

135 Maverick Fisher to Lewis Fisher, July 7, 2025.

136 Minutes, Oct. 7, 1991, Oct. 7, 1996; *News*, Summer 1992. As the Men's Garden Club was joined by members of the Master Gardeners and other groups, new leaders of the Children's Vegetable Garden program included Col. Joe Miller, James Alford, and Joe Van Bibber.

137 Minutes, July 8, 1985; Bill Cunningham, "Xeriscape Project Slated," *Express*, Aug. 24, 1984, 3-B. In mid-1985 the staff collected plants in Arizona and attended a plant conservation meeting in Washington, DC, and a national botanical garden association meeting in Philadelphia. Some took a society-sponsored two-week garden tour of England that netted $1,700 for the society. That fall the botanical garden used $280,000 in city funding to build backup potting sheds, maintenance barns, and a greenhouse. *Minutes*, Sept. 9, 1985.

138 "Regal Regency," *Light*, June 23, 1982; Carol Barnes, "Ochse Wins Extension," *Times*, July 1, 1982; Minutes, Aug. 16, 1982. Ochse was the former owner of the St. Anthony Hotel and one of two developers of housing along that side of Funston Place forty years earlier.

139 San Antonio Botanical Society to Board of Adjustment, Aug. 25, 1982, SAPL; Director, Department of Parks and Recreation, to Department of Building Inspections, Aug. 25, 1982, SAPL. *Times*: John Jeter, "SA Board Axes," Sept. 2, 1982, 1; Doris Dixon, "Ochse Denied," Apr. 19, 1983, 2.

140 Minutes, Jan. 6, Feb. 3, Apr. 14, 1986.

141 Minutes, Feb. 3, 1986.

142 Rex C. Moyer and the San Antonio Botanical Society, "Mahncke Park Arboretum, a Planned Multi-Purpose Urban San Antonio Facility" (1991), SABG. An estimated eighty-six trees were in poor condition or dying and unlikely to be replaced by new growth, as, in the decades since the park began to be maintained, the mowing schedule prevented natural reseeding of trees. Trees in Freedom Grove were not included in the inventory.

143 Moyer and Botanical Society, "Mahncke Park Arboretum."

144 Moyer and Botanical Society, "Mahncke Park Arboretum"; Minutes, Dec. 5, 1988, Apr. 3, 1989, Aug. 5, 1991. The long-range planning committee also approved investigating acquisition of the underused Lamar Elementary School, facing Mahncke Park's northern side, to be the arboretum's educational center, with a library, herbarium, and classrooms. The playground would be preserved for neighborhood use. Minutes, Oct. 4, 1993.

145 Minutes, Mar. 2, Oct. 5, 1987; Beryl B. Simpson to Rex Moyer, Aug. 8, 1991, SABG.

146 Minutes, Mar. 7, 1988, Aug. 5, 1991, Jan. 6, 1992, Oct. 4, 1993.

Kumamoto En and a Carriage House

147 Vicki Vaughan, "Shirane Helped S.A. Win Businesses," *Express*, June 19, 2013. The state of Texas also joined the promotion. Seiichi Shirane died in 1990.

148 Pat Williams, "Japanese Garden Plans," *Express*, Oct. 10, 1988, 1-A; Minutes, Feb. 7, July 11, Nov. 7, 1994. The Yasuimoko Koumeten Company Ltd. architectural and construction company in Kyoto had been in Yasui's family since the seventeenth century. Since 1987 Kumamoto's population has risen from 470,000 to more than 730,000.

149 "East Meets West," *Express*, Apr. 29, 2000, 1-E.

150 "The Kumamoto En," *News* (Summer 1989); "East Meets West," *Express*, Apr. 29, 2000, 1-E; Donnie Pylant, "Kumamoto En," Japanese Garden Reference Library, North American Japanese Garden Association, Apr. 13, 2012, https://najga.org/kumamoto-en, retrieved May 31, 2025.

151 "East Meets West," *Express*, Apr. 29, 2000, 1-E; "Information on Kumamoto En Japanese Garden," SABG, n.d., 1–8.

152 "East Meets West," *Express*, Apr. 29, 2000, 1-E.

153 Pylant, "Kumamoto En."

154 "Kumamoto En," *News* (Summer 1989).

155 "Director's Report," *News* (Summer 1990); "Information on Kumamoto En Japanese Garden," SABG, 1–8. One entry fence was in Katsura style, its bamboo stems in wooden frames set on a narrow layer of stone for protection from the soil. The Otsu-style fence's vertical bamboo strips alternated in groups of three between widely spaced rows of two. The Kenninji fence featured wood-framed vertical slats with ornately scalloped diagonal braces on the garden side. The fourth fence, in Daimyo/Shogun style, was set on a knee-high wall of stone, its vertical bamboo branches sheared to leave a broomed top and held by chestnut posts and scalloped diagonal supports.

156 "East Meets West," *Express*, Apr. 29, 2000, 1-E.

157 *News*: "Japanese Ambassador" (Spring 2005); "Kumamoto Garden Revitalized" (Winter 2005); "Thank You" (Summer 2008).

158 Minutes, Feb. 27, Nov. 26, 2012; May 28, Aug. 25, 2013.

159 "Specification of Stable & Coach House for D. Sullivan, Esq., San Antonio, Texas," Alfred Giles & Guindon, *Architect* (1896), 1–17, Alexander Architectural Library, University of Texas at Austin. Although undertaken during Giles's brief partnership with Henri E. M. Guindon, Giles himself is credited with the carriage house design. George, *Architectural Legacy*, 111.

160 "Carriage House Renewal," *Light*, Sept. 5, 1984, 9-C; "SAMA Rejects," *Express*, Oct. 17, 1985, 7-H; Minutes, Nov. 26, 2007. Sullivan's daughter Mary Elizabeth, widow of Civil War Union drummer boy and later brigadier general John L. Clem, upon her death in 1967 willed the property to the Catholic Archdiocese of San Antonio. Two years later the archdiocese sold the Sullivan house to the adjacent *San Antonio Light*, which tore it down for a parking lot. David Straus, however, bought the carriage house and planned to restore it as a steak house until plans arose for his Stockman Restaurant on the River Walk. In 1971 Straus sold the carriage house to the *Light* with the stipulation that it could be moved but not demolished.

161 Minutes, Sept. 30, 1996, Nov. 17, 1986. A thorough treatment of the history of the Sullivan property and options for the carriage house is in Stubblefield-Mogas Architects AIA, "Sullivan Carriage House: A Feasibility Study for the City of San Antonio Parks and Recreation Department and the San Antonio Botanical Center," Nov. 17, 1986, SABG.

162 Minutes, Sept. 8, 1987; George, *Architectural Legacy*, 64; City of San Antonio, "Ordinance 65763 Authorizing the San Antonio Botanical Center Society to Relocate the Sullivan Carriage House," Sept. 24, 1987, SABG.

163 "Carriage House," *Express*, Nov. 5, 1987, 3-D.

164 Minutes, Sept. 8, 1987; "Carriage House," *Light*, June 3, 1988, 1-B; Irby Hightower to John Troy, Mar. 1, 1993, SABG.

165 Minutes, Sept. 11, 1989. Although the carriage house had been listed in 1978 on the National Park Service–managed National Register of Historic Places, after the move it was taken off the list because the new setting did not match its original urban environment. Preservation of the exterior was assured, however, with conveyance in 1988 of a facade easement to the San Antonio Conservation Society, a major contributor to the move. Minutes, Jan. 11, Apr. 4, 1988; George, *Architectural Legacy*, 65.

166 *News* (Winter 1991); Minutes, Aug. 3, Sept. 14, 1992; Feb. 1, May 3, July 8, 1993; Jan. 3, Nov. 7, 1994. The need for additional funds to complete new exterior doors was met by a $15,000 grant from the Marcia and Otto Koehler Foundation.

167 Candace Andrews to Lewis Fisher, Sept. 15, 2025.

168 *News*, Fall 1990, Spring 1993, Winter 1995; Minutes, Jan. 3, 1994; George, *Architectural Legacy*, 66.

169 Minutes, Jan. 5, 2005; May 21, May 30, Sept. 24, 2007.

170 *Times*, June 9, 1994; Minutes, June 6, 1994, June 5, 1995.

171 Candace Andrews to Lewis Fisher, Sept. 15, 2005.

The Moy Grande Leads the Way

172 Such tributes to Moy in this chapter by Paul Cox, Eric Tschanz, Jerry Parsons, Robert L. Washington, Harry W. Mazal, Marjie Scharff, and others were written at the time of Moy's retirement in 1999 and are preserved in SABG archives. The archives also include the reports "New Varieties Developed by Ying Doon Moy" (1990–1998 and 1999–2006) and Moy's research reports for 2006 and 2007. Published articles include Marsha M. Harlow and Douglas F. Welsh, "Papa Papaya," *Neil Sperry's Gardens*, June 1998, 41; *News*, Fall 1997, Summer 1999.

173 "City Seeks Patents," *Express*, Nov. 20, 1991, 1-A.

174 Paul Cox, "Ying Doon Moy," manuscript, Dec. 24, 1998, SABG; Harry Mazal, "Ying Doon Moy: A Fond (but Sad) Farewell," manuscript, SABG.

175 Parsons, who frequently advised botanical garden staff, was a Texas A&M University professor in the Department of Horticultural Sciences and head of Texas A&M's Agricultural Extension Service at San Antonio.

176 "City Seeks Patents," *Express*, Nov. 20, 1991, 1-A.

177 Minutes, May 1, 1995.

178 Greg Grant, "Goodbye Mr. Moy," *The Arbor Gate* (blog), Nov. 30, 2012, https://arborgate.com/blog/garden/goodbye-mr-moy, retrieved May 28, 2025.

179 Grant, "Goodbye Mr. Moy."

180 Bradford Lawton to Lewis F. Fisher, Nov. 17, 2025.

181 Minutes, Apr. 4, 1994, Sept. 11, 1995; Jerry M. Parsons, "Another First for Texas," *Neil Sperry's Gardens*, July–August 1995, 33–34; Grant, "Goodbye Mr. Moy."

182 Minutes, Nov. 16, 2004; "*Hedychium 'Dr. Moy*,'" Plant Delights Nursery, www.plantdelights.com/products/hedychium-dr-moy, retrieved June 16, 2025.

183 Leon Macha, "The Hardy Satsuma (Changsat) Story," PLANTanswers, www.plantanswers.com/Articles/TheHardySatsuma.asp, retrieved May 29, 2025.

184 Ying D. Moy, "The Research Report of 2007," manuscript, Jan. 15, 2008, SABG.

185 Candace Andrews to Lewis Fisher, May 27, 2025. Moy's wife, Lisa, was a traditional Chinese doctor and horticulturist. At the time of his retirement their two sons were pursuing graduate degrees in aerospace science, one at Purdue and the other at Princeton.

186 Minutes, Apr. 7, July 7, 1981.

187 Minutes, Nov. 19, 1985; Debbie Benesch, "History of the Center for Plant Conservation Program at San Antonio Botanical Garden," 2012, SABG.

188 *News*, Summer 1988.

189 *News*, Fall 2000.

190 "Center for Plant Conservation," "Rare and Endangered Garden," *Vibrante*, Jan.–Apr. 2023, 6–9.

191 Minutes, Apr. 4, 1994; Center for Plant Conservation Plant Profile, "Walker's Manihot (*Manihot walkerae*)," https://saveplants.org/plant-profile/?CPCNum=2798, retrieved Aug. 15, 2025.

192 Minutes, June 21, 2005; Susan Mooberry to Lewis Fisher, May 7, 2025.

193 "Plant Protectors," *Vibrante*, Jan.–Apr. 2023, 4.

194 "Sowing the Future," *Vibrante*, Jan.–Apr. 2024, 30–33; "The Oak Collection," *Vibrante*, May–Aug. 2024, 27–31; Michael Eason to Lewis Fisher, Sept. 10, 2025.

195 *News*, Summer 1988. An attempt at hot, dry germination of Big Red Sage seed had an 80 percent success rate.

196 "Lost and Found: How Police Search and Rescue Tactics Helped Track Down a Rare Oak," *Guardian*, Nov. 3, 2022, www.theguardian.com/environment/2022/nov/03/lost-and-found-lateleaf-oak-quercus-tardifolia-aoe, retrieved Aug. 15, 2025.

197 Michael Eason to Lewis Fisher, Oct. 14, 2025.

Complications and Renewal

198 "Vandals Plaguing," *Express*, Feb. 20, 1990, 1-A.

199 "Ochse to Consider," *Times*, Sept. 2, 1982, 3; "City Plans Greenbelt," *Express*, Feb. 21, 1990.

200 Minutes, Feb. 27, 1989; "City Plans Greenbelt," *Express*, Feb. 21, 1990.

201 Minutes, Nov. 6, 1989, Oct. 5, 1992. *Express*: "Vandals Plaguing," Feb. 20, 1990, 1-A; "City Plans Greenbelt," Feb. 21, 1990.

202 Minutes, Mar. 23, Apr. 2, 1990; Nov. 7, 1994; Jan. 16, 1995; Sept. 9, 1996; July 6, 2004; July 9, 2007; Jan. 28, 2008. In addition to making major grants, the Ewing Halsell Foundation also made smaller ones, like $1,600 to support the Professional Association for Cactus Development's annual conference held at the garden in 1995. Minutes, Oct. 2, 1995.

203 Minutes, Feb. 1, 1993; Oct. 3, 1994; July 1, Oct. 7, Nov. 4, 1996; Eric Lautzenheiser to Board of Directors, June 19, 1996, SABG; *San Antonio Botanical Garden Master Plan, September 1999*, SAPL, 5. The 1992 preliminary conceptual plan by landscape architects James Keeter and Dixie Watkins and Associates grew into a final conceptual plan by Ford, Powell and Carson, but the landscape architect charged with the project left the firm. Given all the issues, in July 1996 the executive committee, with input from Gilbert Denman Jr., tabled the entire process.

204 *Summary of Enactments: 69th Legislature, Regular and First Called Sessions* (Texas Legislative Council, 1985), chapter 381, 2739.

205 Frank Stromboe Jr. to Wally McGee, Feb. 19, 1997, SABG; Hon. Roger Flores to San Antonio Botanical Society, Aug. 20, 1997, SABG; Minutes, Oct. 2, 1995, Jan. 5, 1998. Rights were released on the Brackenridge Park Golf course ten years later.

206 Minutes, June 7, 1983, Nov. 17, 1986; Gloria Duke-Richter to Harold Hallmark, Oct. 16, 1996, SABG; *News*, Summer 1997.

207 *News*, Summer 2000.

208 *The Texas Native Trail, San Antonio Botanical Garden Interpretive Master Plan*, 6. The $500,000 effort drew grants led by $100,000 each from the SBC, H-E-B, and Zachry Foundations.

209 Minutes, Mar. 1, Sept. 21, 2004; Jan. 5, Oct. 18, 2005; Apr. 24, 2006; *Texas Native Trail*, 20–23; *News* (Summer 2006).

210 Minutes, Apr. 23, May 21, 2007; Aug. 24, 2009.

211 Minutes, Apr. 26, 2010.

212 Candace Andrews to Lewis Fisher, Aug. 14, 2025. Added were a membership director and a development director plus, after that, a financial officer.

213 "Center Eyed," *Times*, Mar. 8, 1990, 1; Minutes, Oct. 3, 1994, July 10, 1995, Feb. 25, 2013.

214 Minutes, Jan. 3, July 11, 1994; Oct. 2, 1995; Jan. 8, 1996. Friedrich Wilderness Park has since grown to six hundred acres with ten miles of hiking trails. In addition to running Friedrich Wilderness Park, the garden staff was tasked with managing Mahncke Park's Freedom Grove, directly across from the San Antonio Garden Center, and the three-acre "Mueller Estate" on South Probandt Street, on which no further information is available. Garden staff also briefly managed Brackenridge Park's declining Japanese Tea Garden prior to its restoration in 2005.

215 One highly qualified candidate with a background in directing gardens in subtropical climates declined in 1989 based on the offered salary. Minutes, Sept. 11, 1989.

216 Susan Lane to Lewis F. Fisher, Oct. 6, 2025.

217 Ad Hoc Committee memorandums, Aug. 26, 1997, Jan. 27, 1998, SABG; Minutes, Apr. 4, Apr. 12, 2004.

218 Minutes, Feb. 4, Apr. 12, 2004.

219 Minutes, Feb. 4, Mar. 1, Apr. 12, Oct. 23, 2006; grant agreement, 2005, SABG.

220 Minutes, Oct. 19, 2004.

A Lively Place

221 In 2006 some distant visitors were delegations from the American Orchid Society, the Mexico National Federation of Garden Clubs, the Moscow Botanical Garden, and seventeen other organizations.

222 Candace Andrews to Lewis F. Fisher, Sept. 15, 2025.

223 "Imaginary Worlds," *Vibrante*, May–Aug. 2023, 4–11.

224 Minutes, Nov. 9, 2021; "SAWS Sponsors," *Times*, Apr. 22, 2004, 12; "Vision of Sustainability," *Vibrante*, Sept.–Dec. 2023, 23–31.

225 Paul Schattenberg, "Incredible Edible Insect Event in San Antonio a 'Tasteful' Experience," Texas A&M AgriLife Center at Uvalde, Oct. 29, 2018, https://uvalde.tamu.edu/2018/10/29/incredible-edible-insect-event-in-san-antonio-a-tasteful-experience, retrieved July 28, 2025.

226 Minutes, Feb. 22, 2010; Feb. 28, Mar. 28, 2011; Nov. 15, 2022. The late Mary Irish's books include *Gardening on the Dry Side of Texas: Drought-Tolerant Plants and Techniques* (Texas A&M Press, 2025).

227 Minutes, Feb. 27, June 26, 2017; Aug. 18, 2020.

228 Minutes, June 7, Oct. 19, Nov. 16, 2004; Feb. 15, June 21, 2005; Jan. 26, 2006; Jan. 24, 2011.

229 Minutes, Apr. 23, June 30, Aug. 8, 2008; Apr. 27, Feb. 23, May 26, 2009; Apr. 26, 2010. In 2012 power lines were removed and cable lines relocated, terminating all easements along the closed street. The city straightened the tract by removing a curved intersection near the former Funston Place and Old Austin Road in 2013. Minutes, June 12, 2012, Dec. 2, 2013.

Independent at Last

230 Candace Andrews left in 2017 to chair the board of the Cibolo Preserve in Boerne.

231 Minutes, Mar. 8, 2007; Oct. 26, 2009; July 26, Oct. 25, 2010; Aug. 10, 2016; June 25, Aug. 27, 2018; "San Antonio Botanical Gardens Agreement," City Ordinance No. 2010-10-21-0929, Oct. 21, 2010, SABG.

232 Minutes, Feb. 25, 2008, Jan. 25, 2009.

233 Paths wound past a picnic area and a dry creek bed reminiscent of the Texas Hill Country, filled with rocks for children to play with. There were also a pecan grove with a small amphitheater, a spring, a theater with an array of tree stumps to sit on, the inch-deep Greehey Family Foundation No Name Creek, and Muhly Maze, with four-foot ornamental Muhly grasses. Near the end of the path one could climb Semmes Prickly Pear Peak to an ivy-covered shelter for a view of the city.

234 Adrienne Jordan, "The 8 Most Beautifully Designed Botanical Gardens in America," *Architectural Digest*, Mar. 14, 2019; "AIA Architecture Award 2024," AIA, June 7, 2024, www.aia.org/design-excellence/award-winners/architecture-award-2024, retrieved July 10, 2025.

235 Melinda Cerda, a Parks and Recreation Department administrator, was interim director for ten months, then former board president Mary Ann Beach, who headed the search for the new director. A memorial service was held in the amphitheater in June 2019 for retiree Paul Cox, sixty-six, who started at the garden before its opening in 1980 and served three times as interim director for a total of seven years. A reception at the Auld House followed the memorial service.

236 Minutes, Jan. 25, 2022.

237 Minutes, Jan. 21, 2025.

238 "Old Time Wooden Nickel Co.," www.ot-wooden-nickel.com/memorial-page, retrieved Oct. 3, 2025. The company gained the distinction of being "the only wooden nickel manufacturer to offer wooden nickels with a full color imprint." In 2002 the "World's Largest Wooden Nickel," 13.5 feet in diameter, was unveiled at the company museum. Four years later the title was claimed by a new wooden sculpture 16 feet in diameter in Iowa City, Iowa.

239 "San Antonio Botanical Garden," *Express*, Aug. 19, 2023. Funding in the amount of $5 million came from Tax Increment Reinvestment Zone funds, $2.5 million from city bonds approved in 2022, and $800,000 from the botanical society.

240 Betje Black Klier, "François Guilbeau, Jr.," *Handbook of Texas Online*, updated Sept. 20, 2016, www.tshaonline.org/handbook/entries/guilbeau-francois-jr, retrieved August 17, 2025. Having sold the four-acre reservoir site to the San Antonio Water Works Company, a few months later Guilbeau sold adjoining land to George Brackenridge, who conveyed it to the city for the portion of Mahncke Park now occupied by the garden. Andrew Labay confirmed that soil on the vineyard's site could nurture vines of the types sent to France. Andrew Labay to Lewis F. Fisher, Oct. 6, 2025.

Selected Bibliography

Black, Stephen L. *An Historical and Archaeological Assessment of the Proposed San Antonio Botanical Center.* Center for Archaeological Research, University of Texas at San Antonio, Archaeological Survey Report No. 24, 1976.

City of San Antonio Parks and Recreation Department Archives. San Antonio Public Library, Texana Room.

Fisher, Lewis F. *Brackenridge: San Antonio's Acclaimed Urban Park.* Trinity University Press, 2022.

———. *Saving San Antonio: The Preservation of a Heritage.* 2nd ed. Trinity University Press, 2016.

George, Mary Carolyn. *The Architectural Legacy of Alfred Giles.* Trinity University Press, 2006.

Johnson, David R. *In the Loop: A Political and Economic History of San Antonio.* Trinity University Press, 2020.

McLean, Bert J. *The Romance of San Antonio's Water Supply and Distribution.* Water Supply Co., 1927.

News from the Botanical Garden. San Antonio Botanical Society, 1986–2000.

News from the San Antonio Botanical Garden. San Antonio Botanical Society, 2001–19.

Quillin, Ellen Schulz, and Bess Woolford. *The Story of the Witte Memorial Museum, 1922–1960.* San Antonio Museum Association, 1966.

San Antonio Botanical Garden 2010 Master Site Plan. Dallas: MESA, 2010.

San Antonio Botanical Garden Archives, San Antonio Botanical Garden.

San Antonio Botanical Society Minutes. Board of directors and executive committee meetings, 1982–96, 1997–99,* 2003,* 2004–25, San Antonio Botanical Garden. (* incomplete)

Sibley, Marilyn McAdams. *George W. Brackenridge: Maverick Philanthropist.* University of Texas Press, 1973.

Vibrante, the Member Magazine of the San Antonio Botanical Garden. San Antonio Botanical Garden, 2020–25.

Witlinger, J. Mark, coordinator. *San Antono Botanical Garden Master Plan September 1999.* Park Design and Project Services, San Antonio Parks and Recreation Department, 1999.

Credits

Emilio Ambasz, x, xii (left), xvi (lower left)
Bexar County Deed Records, 9, 206, 13 (top left); 105, 19, 16
Bill Fisher, xiii (top), 53
Lewis F. Fisher, ii, xvi (top and lower right), xvii (right), xiii (middle and below), 4, 5, 9, 15, 18, 23, 38 (below), 44, 56 (top left), 59, 78, 79 (right), 87, 93 (lower right), 94 (top left and lower left), 96 (top right), 99 (lower right)
Mary M. Fisher, vi, xii (right), xvii (left), 38 (above), 50, 70 (below), 72, 74, 77 (lower right), 79 (left), 83, 85, 96 (left and two lower), 97, 98, 116
Maverick Fisher, 86 (left)
Fort Sam Houston Military Museum, 15 (top), 24
Robert Holliday, 69
National Archives, NAID 364424089, 12
Maria Watson Pfeiffer, 16
San Antonio Botanical Garden, xiv, xv, xviii (upper three), xx–1, 10, 35 (right), 36 (top), 40, 42, 43, 45 (below), 46, 52 (top left, lower right), 54, 58, 60-61, 65, 66, 68, 71, 75, 76, 77 (top, lower left), 80, 81, 82, 84, 86 (right), 88, 92, 94 (right), 95 (two lower), 99 (top two), 100, 101
San Antonio Express, 20
San Antonio Express-News/ZUMA Press Wire, xiii (top), xviii (lower right), xix (below), 7, 25, 26–27, 32, 33, 34, 35 (left), 36 (lower), 45 (top), 47, 49, 52 (top right), 53, 56 (lower left, right), 64, 67, 73
San Antonio Public Library, Texana/Genealogy Collections, xix (top), 21, 39
San Antonio Water System, 22
Bill Timmerman, 90, 93 (top two and lower left), 95 (top two)
U.S. Botanic Garden, 70 (top)
University of Texas at San Antonio Special Collections, xviii (below), xix (below), 7, 13 (right, two lower left), 26–27, 33, 34, 36 (lower), 47, 49, 52 (top right), 56 (lower left, right), 64
University of Texas Libraries, Alexander Architectural Archives, University of Texas at Austin, Alfred Giles Collection, 55; Stewart King Collection, 30

Index

Adobe house, 38
Akhil, Omar, 95
Alexander, Claire, 80–81
Ambasz, Emilio, xii–xiii, xviii–xix, 103n15
Andrews, Candace, 67, 79, 80, 91
Arboretum, 30, 31, 48–49, 106n91, 107n142, 107n144
Art in the Garden, 84–86
Auld house, 39, 41, 75, 76,

Beach, Mary Ann, 110n235
Beautify San Antonio Association, 31–32
Bees, 69–70
Bexar County Extension Service, 48
Bird Watch, Lende, 78
Bishop, Louis P., 42
Botanical gardens elsewhere, xii, xiii, xiv, 3–4, 42, 107n122; Europe, xii, 3
Brackenridge, George W., 4, 13, 14–15, 17, 105n72; boulevard plan, 20–23; donates Mahncke Park, 19–22, 105n69, 110n240; botanical garden plan, 4; alcoholic beverage prohibition, 42, 74–76, 109n205
Brackenridge Park, 4–5, 6, 11, 15, 20, 21–22, 23, 38, 64; Japanese Tea Garden, 109n214
Brackman, Bob, 80, 81, 83, 91, 95
Carr, Sabina, 95, 97
Carriage House, Sullivan, 55–59, 74, 88, 108n159–61, 108n165–66
Cavanaugh, Thomas, 12, 14
Center for Archaeological Research, University of Texas at San Antonio, 34
Center for Plant Conservation, U.S. Fish and Wildlife Service, 67, 69, 71
Cerda, Melinda, 110n235
Chamberlain Investment Company, 16–17, 105n62–63
Children's Vegetable Garden, 31, 46–47, 84, 95, 107n136
Chisos Mountains oak, 70–71
Cisneros, Henry, 51, 54, 103n16
City Water Board, 24–25
Cockrell, Lila 8–9, 49, 54
Conservation Society of San Antonio, 108n165
Conservatory, first plan, 35, 45
Conservatory, Lucile Halsell, 79, 81, 86, 89, 99, 110n239; conception and design, xi, xii, xv–xviii; construction, xi–xviii; dedication and opening, xvii–xix, 103n15; architectural critiques and awards, xiii, xv–xix; plant collection and placement, xiv–xvii; vandalism, 73, 89; alpine garden, xv; exhibition room, xvii; fern room, xvi; Gretchen Northrup Tropical Pavilion, xiv, xvii, 103n8i; Kleberg Desert Pavilion, xiv, xvii, 103n8; Napier Orchid Pavilion, 99; orangery, xvii; Palm House, xvi–xvii, 89, 100
Cook, George C., 31, 33, 34
Cox, Paul, xiv–xv, 37, 54, 64, 68–69, 73, 79, 80, 110n235
Culinary Garden, Zachry Foundation, 93
Culinary Pavilion, Goldsbury Foundation, 93

Darner, Ronald, 31, 42, 48, 107n123–24
Deely, Margaret, 42, 59
Deely, Pat, xviii
Denman, Gilbert, Jr., 32–33, 36, 45, 48, 49, 81, 100, 107n124, 109n203; impact on garden, viii, xi, 32, 33, 41; arboretum, 48–49; conservatory, xi–xiii, xvii–xviii; Funston Place addition, 74; Sullivan Carriage House, 57; Texas Native Area, 33, 36
Dinosaurus Tex, 82–83
Discovery Center, H-E-B, 93
Display Garden, Mays Family, 93
Downey, Robert, 59
Dry Rock Creek, Joan and Herb Kelleher Foundation, 94

Duke-Richter, Gloria, 78

Eason, Michael, 69, 70–71, 98
East Texas farmstead, 36–37, 46, 89
East Texas lake, 21, 36, 77–78, 86, 88, 89, 105n71
Edwards Aquifer, 14, 15, 105n57
Edwards Underground Water Authority, 48
Emerson, Jon S., 76
Entrance building, 35, 42, 43
Erben, Joel, 89
Erickson, Katie, 86, 96–97
Event Center, Betty Kelso, 92, 94–95
Events, 46, 83–86, 88, 96–97. *See also* Art in the Garden, *Dinosaurus Tex*, Gardens by Moonlight, Viva Botanica
Ewing Halsell Foundation, 32–33, 36, 37–38, 42, 48, 73, 81, 93, 100, 103n7, 109n202; conservatory, xi, xiii–xiv, xvii, 81, 89; Funston Place addition, 73–74

Family Adventure Garden, 3, 93–94, 110n233; Greehey Family Foundation No Name Creek, 95, 110n233; Semmes Prickly Pear Peak, 3, 34, 110n233
Fisher, Lewis S., 107n128
Ford, O'Neil, 8, 31
Fort Sam Houston, 6, 9, 14, 17, 22–23, 24, 73, 98, 105n55
Fountain Plaza, 29, 35, 36, 41, 42, 43, 94
Fraser, Robert, 8, 31
Freedom Grove, 48, 49, 109n214
Friedrich Wilderness Park, 79–80, 109n214
Fromme, Tres, 88

Funston Place addition, 22, 24, 73–74, 89, 91–94, 110n229

Garden Club of America, 6
Garden for the Blind, 34, 35–36, 64
Gardens by Moonlight, 84–86
Garison, Cathy, 76, 83
Gazebo, 34–35, 41. *see also* Tempietto
Gaydos, Steve, xiv–xv
Gift shop, 43, 45, 58, 93
Grant, Greg, 65
Greenhouses, xv, 45, 65, 69, 70, 99, 107n137
Greenwood, Jim, 93
Greenwood, Karen, 92–93
Guilbeau, François, Jr., 12, 13, 100, 110n240

Hammond, Hall, xiii, 42, 45
HemisFair, 8
Heritage gardens, 64, 96
Hightower, Irby, 57
Hill Country area, 38–39, 76
Hogan, Helen, xviii, 57
Hogg, Sam, 89, 99
Hughes, Betty, 45
Hunt, Curtis, 57
Huntington, 69

Irish, Mary, 88

Japanese Garden. *See* Kumamoto En

Kearney, Elaine, 86–88
Keeter, James E., 30, 31, 33, 34, 39, 47, 109n203
Kenny, Toney, 68
King, Stewart, 30–31
Krisch, Rudy, III, 37
Kumamoto En, 51–54, 74, 88–89, 108n155

Labay, Andrew, 31, 37, 98, 99, 110n240
LaCoste, Jean Batiste, 11–14
Lake, Sarah, 76
Lamar Elementary School, 24, 25, 107n144
Lambert, Ray, 23
Lane, Susan, 80, 81
Lautzenheiser, Eric, 66, 80
Lawson, Marline, 93
Litchke, Scott, 67, 78
Logo, 45, 65–66, 100
Longwood Gardens, 69

Mahncke, Ludwig, 20, 21; monument, 29, 106n85
Mahncke Park, 6, 8, 24, 42; boulevard plan, 19–23, 105n69; establishment, 20–22; neglected, 23–24, 29; efforts to dismember, 9, 23–25, 106n77; *see also* Arboretum, San Antonio Botanical Garden
Mahncke Park Neighborhood Association, 48, 89
Martin, Graham, 78
Master plans, 31, 48, 49, 73, 74, 92, 98–99, 109n203
Matthews, Malcolm, 81
Mays, Marie and Ryan, 99
Mazal, Harry, 64, 65
McAlpin, Bruce, xiii, 42
McGee, Wally, 76, 88
Men's Garden Club, 7, 46
Miller, Phil, 98
Mogas, Richard, 57
Moy, Ying Doon, 63–67, 108n172, 109n185

Moy Grande, 63, 65–66
Moyer, Rex, 48–49
Murphy, Lucretia, 6, 42, 104n32

Napier, Dacia and Lanham, 98
National Seed Storage Laboratory, 67–68
Northrup, Gretchen, 42

Ochse, William, Jr., 24, 48, 107n138

Palisado home, 38
Pape Construction Company, 57
Pape-Dawson Engineers, 92
Pasztor, Patty Leslie, 67, 68
Parsons, Jerry, 65, 66, 67, 108n175

Rare and Endangered Garden, xiv, 69
Reed Hilderbrand, 98
Rehler, Ken, 76
Reservoir/amphitheater, xi, 11, 20–21, 24, 29, 105n69, 110n240; construction and initial use, 12–17, 104n47–48, 104n52, 105n55; amphitheater, 11, 35, 84
Richmond, Jack and Laura, 57

San Antonio Botanical Center. *See* San Antonio Botanical Garden
San Antonio Botanical Garden, early efforts to establish, 3–9, 104n37; goals, xi, 42, 45; site selection and preparation, xi, 8, 25, 29–31, 34–39; groundbreaking and opening, xi, 34, 41, 107n122; opposes developments, 48; attendance, 83, 96–97, 110n221; independent operation, 91; bond issue funding, 5, 31, 92, 110n239; climate and soil, xii–xiii, 31, 37, 38, 110n240; plant conservation/sales and innovations, 64–72, 88, 109n195; *see also* San Antonio Garden Center, sponsors
San Antonio Botanical Society, 41, 42, 78–81, 91, 107n125, 109n212
San Antonio Business and Professional Women's Club, 6, 24
San Antonio Garden Center, 6–9, 11, 25, 29, 35, 49, 103–04n31, 104n35, 104n43–44, 109n214; sponsors botanical garden, 8–9, 25, 30–31, 34–35, 41, 42, 107n123
San Antonio River Authority, 48, 88
San Antonio Shooting Company/Schuetzen Verein, 17, 105n64
San Antonio Water System, 86–88
San Antonio Water Works Company, 11–15, 104n47–48, 104n52, 105n55–57
San Pedro Springs Park, 3, 8
Scanlan, Bill, 99
Schumacher house, 39, 41, 44, 45, 99, 107n128
Science and Education Committee, 48, 67, 69
Sensory Garden. *See* Garden for the Blind
Shirane, Naoko, 51, 54
SO–IL, 99
Steves, Patsy, 42
Stockdale, Dave, 80
Stumberg, Mary Pat, 89

Tempietto, xiii, xiv, 35. *See also* Gazebo
Ten Eyck, Christine, 92
Texas Native Area. *See* Texas Native Trail
Texas Native Trail, 33, 36–39, 41, 74–78, 109n208
Texas snowbell, 68
Thomas, David, 46–47
TREES (Texas Recovery for Ecological and Environmental Stability), 98
Trinity University, xviii, 48, 80
Troy, John, 74, 76
Trumble, Katherine, viii, 95, 97–98, 99
Tschanz, Eric, xiv, 45, 80

University of Texas, 22, 36, 74–76

Viva Botanica, 46, 65, 66, 84

Washington, Robert, 42, 57, 81
Washington Heights, 11, 16–17, 105n65
Washington Heights Improvement Company, 17, 22
WaterSaver Community, 69, 86–88
WaterSaver Garden, Kyse, 88
Weddle, Philip, 92
Welcome Building, Halsell, 93
Weniger, Delbert, 67
Wigodsky, Dan, 103n8
Wilkinson, Julie, 99
Witt, Harriet, 6, 103–04n31
Witte Museum, 6–7, 57, 103–04n31, 104n37
Wooden Nickel Company, Old Time, 98, 110n238
Wrockloff, Beth, 88

Xeriscape, 47, 86. *See also* WaterSaver Community

Yasui, Kiyoshi, 51, 52, 108n148

Zachry, Nancy, 81, 83, 89
Zachry Construction Company, H.B., 36, 65, 78

Lewis F. Fisher is the author of numerous books about San Antonio and Texas, among them *American Venice: The Epic Story of San Antonio's River*, *Saving San Antonio: The Preservation of a Heritage*, *Brackenridge: San Antonio's Acclaimed Urban Park*, *Chili Queens, Haywagons and Fandangos: The Spanish Plazas in Frontier San Antonio*, and *Maverick: The American Name That Became a Legend*. He has received numerous local, state, and national awards. He was named a Texas Preservation Hero by the Conservation Society of San Antonio in 2014 and is a fellow of the Texas State Historical Association.

Barney L. Lipscomb, a leading Texas botanist, is a senior staff member at the Fort Worth Botanic Garden and directs the Texas Floras Project, which documents plant life in the state. He has coauthored three books on state and regional floras and is a member of the board of the Flora of North America Association.